The Flying Smart Handbook

**The Airline Captains' Complete Guide for Passenger Travel
1998 — 1999 Domestic US Edition**

Denis C. Horgan

First Edition

FSH Publishing, Key West, Florida

The Flying Smart Handbook
The Airline Captains' Complete Guide for Passenger Travel
1998 -1999 Domestic US Edition

By Denis C. Horgan

Published by:

FSH Publishing
Post Office Box 4293
Key West, FL 33041-4293 U.S.A.

Copyright© 1998
by Denis C. Horgan
First Printing 1997
Printed in the United States of America

Library of Congress Catalog Card Number: 97-97086
Horgan, Denis C.
    The flying smart handbook: the airline captains' complete guide for passenger air travel / by Denis C. Horgan. — 1st ed.

10 9 8 7 6 5 4 3 2 1

ISBN 0-9661264-0-8 (pbk.)

ABOUT THE COVER

Market demand has sized, shaped and launched the newest member of the Boeing family, the 777. The airplane design offers features, innovations and approaches to aircraft development that set the standard for delivering value to airlines. The 777 the world's largest twinjet—is available in three models: An initial model, a 777-200 increased gross weight (IGW, longer-range) model, and a larger 777-300 model.

The Boeing 777 airplane took its first flight on June 12, 1994, entering the most extensive flight testing effort in commercial aviation history. This resulted in a reliable, service ready airplane that performs as expected upon delivery.

First delivery of the 777 was on May 15, 1995.

As of September 30, 1997, Boeing had delivered 94 777s to 14 customers worldwide.

They are (in order of first delivery): United Airlines, British Airways, All Nippon Airways, China

Southern, Emirates, Thai Airways, Cathay Pacific, Japan Airlines, Japan Air Systems, Korean Air, Malaysia Airlines, Singapore Airlines, Egyptair and Lauda-air.

As of September 30, 1997, Boeing had announced orders for 335 777s from 25 customers worldwide. They are (alphabetically): Air China, Air France, All Nippon Airways, American Airlines, Asiana, British Airways, Cathay Pacific, China Southern, Continental Airlines, Egyptair, Emirates, Garuda Indonesia, GECAS, ILFC, Japan Air System, Japan Airlines, Korean Air, Kuwait Airways, Lauda-air, Malaysia Airlines, Saudia, Singapore Airlines, South African Airways, Thai Airways and United Airlines.

Author's Note: I flew several Boeing Jet Transports as a commercial pilot, and as a Check Airman/Flight Instructor trained hundreds of pilots. Beyond a doubt, Boeing designs and manufactures the finest flying machine in the air.

Table of Contents

About The Author

Captain Horgan started his aviation career as a teenager. Raised in the Bronx, he observed airliners taking off and landing at New York's La Guardia Airport and the Pan American Clipper Flying Boats landing and taking off in the Long Island Sound under the Bronx Whitestone Bridge.

He took his first flying lesson at the age of 14 in a 65-hp seaplane. The thrill and excitement of the first flight set in motion his desire to be an airline pilot. He soloed in five hours and earned his Private Pilots License at age 17.

He served in the United States Marine Corps for five years where he had the opportunity to fly several types of aircraft. Discharged in 1957 he resumed his career in commercial aviation that included flight instruction, charter flights, and employment with American Airlines Reservations.

Hired in 1964 by Allegheny Airlines/US Airways, he remained there until retirement in 1992. During that period he experienced four airline acquisitions, Lake Central, Mohawk, PSA and Piedmont.

While with US Airways he piloted many types of aircraft, including propeller driven piston engine aircraft and the most modern jet powered aircraft. He served as a jet flight instructor and was involved in public relations.

Acknowledgments

I sincerely thank the kind and considerate professionals of the Travel Agent Industry whom, without their expert knowledge this Handbook could not have been written.

I would specially like to thank Laura Myers, (Bureau Chief), *Travel Agent Magazine* and Dan Poynter, Author and Publisher of *The Self Publishing Manual* for their advice and encouragement that made writing this Handbook possible. A very special thanks to Richard Schleh, Public Relations, and Anka Dolecki, International Communication Specialist, The Boeing Commercial Airplane Group, Stacy H. Small (Senior Editor) Airlines, *Travel Agent Magazine*, Kay Shauberger, Anita Travel, St. Petersburg FL, John Hawks and Pat Funk, Association of Retail Travel Agents, Melanie Moore, Uniglobe Travel International, Gayle Martz, Sherpa Pet Trading Company, Jodi Viola, International Airlines Travel Agent Network, Janet Drago and Eric Ardolino, American Society of Travel Agents, Bruno Gallace, Stephen D. Cherry, Roberto Fioravanti and Capt. Ed Kertz.

Edited by Diane Marcou, St. Petersburg, FL

Cover and Book layout by Capt. Arnold Atkatz. Retired from US Airways after 33 years of service where he flew Internationally. He held managerial positions including Instructor and Check Airman.

Warning - Disclaimer

This book is designed to provide information in regard to the subject matter covered. It is sold with the understanding that the publisher and author are not engaged in rendering legal, accounting or other professional services. If legal or other expert assistance is required, the services of a competent professional should be sought.

It is not the purpose of this handbook to reprint all the information that is otherwise available to the author and/or publisher, but to complement, amplify and supplement other texts. You are urged to read all the available material, learn as much as possible about flying smart and to tailor the information to your individual needs.

Every effort has been made to make this handbook as complete and as accurate as possible. However there may be mistakes both typographical and in content. Therefore, this handbook should be used only as a general guide and not as the ultimate source of airline passenger reference. Furthermore, this handbook contains information on airline passenger travel only up to the printing date.

The purpose of this handbook is to educate and entertain. The author and publisher shall have neither liability nor responsibility to any person or entity with respect to any loss or damage caused, directly or indirectly by the information contained in this book.

If you do not wish to be bound by the above, you may return this book to the publisher for a full refund.

IN THE
BEGINNING

Conversation between Orville and Wilbur Wright shortly after the first airplane flight at Kitty Hawk, North Carolina. Thursday, December 17, 1903, 10:35 A.M.

Orville, I know you were in the air for only 12 seconds. So what's my luggage doing in Cleveland?

Author Unknown

Introduction

"What do you mean I don't have a reservation?" "Someone is sitting in my seat!" "You call this food?" "I saw my bag outside the airplane on a cart and they didn't put it on the airplane!" "Why can't I hang my bag in the closet? I'll make it fit!" "I can get my suitcase in the overhead compartment, just help me push the door shut!" "That's the roughest flight I've ever been on!" "Who made that landing, the flight attendant?" "What do you mean my flight is delayed?" "Why can't you get another airplane?" "You canceled my flight, so how come I don't have a reservation on the next flight?" "I'll never fly this airline again!"

Sound familiar?

After flying for a major airline for 30 years and some 30,000 hours in the air, I have seen and heard passengers who were totally frustrated with this transportation system known as Flying. Fortunately, as a pilot I was insulated from the irate passengers by a locked cockpit door. Some days I'd witness a passenger who was just beginning his or her trip experiencing problems at the curbside baggage checking area or at the ticket counter. I'd think, *What a terrible way to start what is meant to be an enjoyable, stress free flight.* Hearing them complain was frustrating to me as an airline Captain who strove to give passengers a safe, comfortable, on-time flight.

Most of the problems and the stress produced by them could have been avoided if the traveling public was made aware of the inner workings of the airline travel industry;

The FLYING SMART Handbook offers that information.

Come Fly with ME, Step by Step. From making your reservation, through the takeoff and landing, to claiming your luggage at your destination.

Have a safe and carefree flight.

1

Making a Reservation

Well it's time to make the reservation for that business or personal trip. This should be relatively simple. Just pick up the phone and call the airline.

What did that recording say? I'll dial it again. O.K. press one for domestic flights, now press four for a flight within the next six days. They're busy, so I'll hold for the next available reservation agent. Nice music. What's that? A real person. Oh, you don't fly to that city? Thank you, I'll call another airline. Now, that only took eleven minutes.

All right. I finally have my reservation although I had to call five airlines before I found one that flew to Altoona.

Why would anyone in today's computerized, active society subject themselves to these time consuming, stress producing delays? There has to be an easier way. And there is.

This year the airline industry projects that some 800 million passengers will board an aircraft in the United States - over two million passengers a day. I recently called five major airlines and experienced delays of twenty-five minutes. They varied from a high of eleven minutes to a low of one. For the record, the airline with the lowest holding time was, I'm sad to say, not my previous employer.

I then telephoned seven Travel Agencies that I randomly selected from the local Yellow Pages. All seven answered by the fourth ring. Based on these comparisons, it's difficult for me to comprehend why anyone subjects himself or herself to the delays encountered attempting to make a reservation through an airline. The obvious solution is;

Call Your Travel Agent.

Travel agents are conveniently located to most travelers, offer personalized service, and are attentive to all your travel needs. I personally would much rather sit eye to eye with the person making my travel arrangements, in a comfortable climate controlled office, than sit or walk around holding a telephone waiting for an airline agent to answer. Most travel agents started their careers as sales agents with the major airlines, which allows them the added luxury of being familiar with the inner workings of the airlines. It is interesting to note that many large companies have their own in-house travel departments or use a particular travel agency to handle all their travel needs.

Airlines will only offer you reservations on their airline. They'll not advise you of better flight times, connecting times or lower fares on competing airlines. Only a travel agent can do this for you. Their computer system displays this information on all participating airlines giving you the best choice of flights and fares. This takes only one call to your local travel agent. Travel agents will look after you if flights change or are cancelled. Call your agent from the airport and have them reschedule you and you won't be competing with 150 other passengers in line at the ticket counter.

Too many travelers are under the impression that travel agents are paid a commission for their services, which is added to the cost of the ticket. Not so. Most of your major airlines pay a fee to the travel agents based on the amount of each ticket.

Unfortunately for passengers, airlines have started a commission war with travel agents. It be gan in February 1995, when Delta Airlines announced a reduction in commissions on all airline tickets of $500 or more from 10% to a set fee of $50 (CAP). As expected other airlines soon followed Delta's lead. Since travel agencies sell 80% of all airline tickets, you can imagine the huge sum the airlines saved by this bold move.

In September 1997, United Airlines, followed shortly thereafter by other airlines, reduced travel agents' commissions again, by a whopping 20%.

The airlines say that this latest reduction in commissions reflects their larger objective of keeping their costs under control.

So what does all this mean to the traveling public? Well, there is no free lunch. If commission reductions continue, travel agents may have to add a service fee to keep *their* costs under control.

But even with a service charge, your ticket probably will be less than if purchased from the airline. Why? Because your travel agent has access to complete, accurate and objective information and the ability to choose the lowest available fare.

Travel Agents offer their clients, at no additional charge, many extras not provided by the airlines. This value-added quality service is what TRAVEL AGENTS are all about.

If you have to pay an extra fee, you will still be getting a bargain.

Notice sometime that most airline advertise-
ments recommend you contact your travel agent or
call the airline. WHY? Travel agents save airlines
hundreds of millions of dollars by performing the service of airline reservation personnel. The airline
doesn't have to construct and staff additional reservation centers. So some of the savings are passed to
the travel agencies as commission.

Your travel agent can issue your ticket and
boarding pass, saving time and inconvenience at the
airport, or you may elect to have your ticket and
boarding pass mailed to you.

Some airlines offer Electronic Ticketing, which
simply means that no ticket will be issued, and you
will not have to worry if you misplace it. You'll go
directly to your flight's boarding gate and present a
valid picture identification issued by a Government
Agency. The gate agent will retrieve your reservation record from their computer and issue you a boarding pass. If flying on an e-ticket, ask your travel agent
or the airline for a copy of your itinerary to carry
with you. The drawback to electronic ticketing is the
delay encountered waiting in line for a boarding pass
at the airport. Also, if your flight is canceled your
reservation must be exchanged for a paper ticket before it will be accepted by another airline and that

means long lines when you usually don't have the time.

Now comes the difficult task of finding the lowest fare available for your particular flight. Airlines change fares on an hourly basis. The odds are in your favor, that if you compared the cost of your ticket with other passengers on your flight, few, if any, would be the same.

Seeking that lowest fare takes the expertise of one who is involved in airline reservations on a daily, hourly basis ---

A professional travel agent.

Since the advent of de-regulation of the airline industry, hundreds of new airlines have appeared in our skies, yet many of them fell by the wayside because of fierce competition exerted by the major pre-deregulation airlines. The few post-deregulation airlines that survived kept pressure on the airline industry to be competitive in their pricing policies. Southwest, America West, and Midway to name a few, have been able to offer attractive low fares. Although most airlines fly the same type modern airliners, offer similar in flight services and flight schedules, low fares are the key to success. This is accomplished by keeping operating costs low.

Total operating expenses include costs of labor, fuel, insurance, aircraft financing, etc., and airlines use a simple formula - Cost per Passenger Seat Mile - to establish their operating cost.

Let's say an airline operates 100 aircraft, each with 100 passenger seats. If the 100 airplanes were to fly one mile, then 10,000 seats would have traveled one mile, or 10,000 seat miles. If the total operating cost to do this is $10,000 then the cost to carry one passenger one mile would be $1.

Airlines operate at between 6 and 12 cents per seat mile, the lower cost representing no frill airlines that traditionally have a much lower pay scale than the higher cost major airlines. To compete and survive in today's market many airlines are seeking wage and benefit concessions from their employees. One major airline facing a strike by its pilots declared bankruptcy, terminated all employee contracts and hired new employees at lower wages.

Consider when making reservation:

♦ *Non-Stop flights if possible.* One air plane nonstop to your destination.

♦ *Direct Flight-Same airplane.* One or more stops.

♦ *Connecting Flight-More than one airplane.* And more than one stop.

When taking a Direct or Connecting flight you

risk the possibility of weather and mechanical delays in-route, causing missed connections and delays. If you can fly non-stop to your destination, do so.

Make your reservation as soon as possible to insure you'll be offered the lowest fare. Remember that special discounted fares usually apply to a predetermined number of seats on a particular flight, sometimes 10% of the aircraft's seating capacity.

Read the fine print. Make sure you understand all the requirements and restrictions. Have your travel agent explain them to you. Once you purchase your ticket, you should not have any surprises.

Check with your travel agent the day before your departure to see if the latest published fare is lower than yours. If so, most airlines will credit you the difference for a future flight. Just present your ticket at the airline ticket counter to receive credit.

Pay by credit card. This is your best form of security in the event of a dispute or flight stoppage by the airline. It's a relatively simple process to obtain a refund or credit through your credit card company.

Select a flight that departs early in the A.M. There's a good chance the aircraft and the crew spent the night there minimizing the chance of a delay.

Select your airline for its routing when making a connection.

You may want to avoid connecting flights in certain geographical locations due to seasonal climatic conditions, for example, Chicago, Denver, Minneapolis, Buffalo, Pittsburgh, Detroit, Cleveland and other cities in the Winter, because of Snow and Ice, as well as Atlanta, Charlotte, Memphis, Cincinnati, Indianapolis, St. Louis and other cities in the Spring and Summer, because of Early Morning Fog.

Summertime flying into tropical weather areas such as Florida, the Caribbean and Central America. For passenger comfort and to avoid in-flight and ground delays, I recommend one should plan to fly in and out of these areas in the early A.M. hours, since thunderstorms usually develop to severe intensity in the afternoon and early evening.

If you require a wheel chair, inform your travel agent of this when making your reservation.

NOTE: When calling airline reservations you feel the agent is discourteous, hang up and call again. Chances of you being connected with the same agent is unlikely.

2

Getting to the Airport

Call the airline to verify your flight departure time before you leave home. If you know your flight has been delayed, you may elect to delay your departure for the airport. If you find your flight has been canceled, you should immediately call your travel agent or airline to see if they have re-scheduled you on a later flight or on another airline. Remember that if your flight is canceled or delayed for several hours, the other passengers will be scurrying to make other reservations, and there may be a limited number of seats available on the next flight.

NOTE: If you are at the airport when your flight cancels, immediately telephone your travel agent or the airline and inform them of your dilemma.

Don't wait to speak to the gate agent. Make alternate reservations. Remember, First Come First Served.

The most common modes of transportation to airports are personal vehicles, airport limousines, taxis and public transportation.

Personal transportation is the most convenient, allowing you to depart at a time that is convenient to you. If you are being driven to the airport you'll have the added luxury of being dropped off at the curbside luggage check in area. **Highly recommended.**

If you intend to park your vehicle in the airport vicinity until you return from your trip, you'll find that several parking choices may be available to you. Generally the most convenient parking is the most expensive. Your airport may offer short and long term parking, short term usually located closest to the terminal, and of course, the most expensive. If your stay will be lengthy you may want to check on off-airport parking. Around the busier airports you will find several of these located just a short distance from the terminal. Some car rentals offer this service. They will take you and your luggage to and from your airline, and their parking rates are usually much lower than at the airport. Remember to allow additional time if you intend to use this service.

Airport limousine service is generally reasonably priced and will take you and your luggage to your airline curbside check-in area. They do have their drawbacks because they usually pick up other passengers in-route, this being time consuming, and you must be ready when they arrive. You must make reservations in advance.

Taxis are convenient but expensive and you are at the mercy of their reliability.

Public transportation is the least expensive but time consuming and not conducive to transporting luggage.

NOTE: when taking transportation other than your own, you must rely on someone else's punctuality. If they're late, you could miss your flight, so allow extra time getting to the airport. If you are late and miss your flight - and have a discounted non-refundable ticket - you may be charged a penalty for your new reservation. If this happens, make sure the airline has not canceled your return flights. This is usually done if you no-show for your origination flight.

3

Checking Luggage and Carry On Items

 I overheard a conversation between a Sky-cap and a passenger checking his luggage at curbside.

> *Passenger* -"I'd like you to check this bag to New York, this one to Los Angeles, this one to Seattle, this one to Miami, and this one to Chicago."
>
> *Skycap* -"Sir, I can't do that. I can only check your bags to your destination, Chicago."
>
> *Passenger* -"Why not? You did it last week!"

There it goes. I'll probably never see it again. I must admit, I've even said this once or twice as I watched my luggage disappear down the conveyor belt. Over the years I've witnessed passengers obviously frustrated when their luggage didn't arrive with them at their destination. Do all you can to see that your baggage is correctly packed, identified and offered to the baggage handler in the best possible condition.

When checking your luggage at the curbside you must present your ticket to the airline representative, the Skycap.

Don't misplace your luggage claim checks. You must have them to make a claim with the airline in the unlikely event your luggage is lost or damaged.

Remember the airline is responsible for checked items only. Liability for all carry-on items is your responsibility.

When using the service of a Skycap it's customary to extend a gratuity of $1.00 per bag. Few Skycaps are employed by the airlines. They are supplied by vendors who contract with the airlines to provide this service. Most of them receive minimum wage and no benefits and depend on tips to augment their salary. Skycaps' current minimum wage is $2.11 per hour.

If not checked curbside, luggage may be checked at the ticket counter. Allow yourself plenty of time for this since there are often long delays while other passengers are accommodated. Luggage may also be checked at the departure gate but this also should be avoided due to intense screening of luggage at security and long lines at the departure gate. Remember Federal Rules governing the number and size of carry-on bags change often and are becoming more restrictive. It appears the day will come when carry-ons will no longer be permitted for safety reasons. Check with your travel agent or airline for limitations.

NOTE: Expensive items that can be readily identified by their outer covering, such as laptop computers, electronic equipment, attache cases, etc., should be packed in suitcases or boxes prior to being checked to avoid the possibility of theft.

For easy identification of your luggage upon arrival at your destination, place some form of personal identification on your luggage such as colored tape, ribbon, etc. Many bags are identical; make sure you have your own bag and not just a look-alike.

Baggage mishandling is a major headache for the airlines, both in cost and loss of the traveling public's confidence in the handling of their personal effects.

The airlines have worked diligently to correct this annoying and preventable problem with increased security and computer tracking.

It appears they have this problem in check. But this is yet another reason to book non-stop flights, which greatly reduce the risk of your luggage being mishandled. The more times your luggage is exposed to connecting flights, the greater the chance of mishandling. If your flight arrives late and you have to run to make your connecting flight, don't be surprised if your luggage doesn't keep up. This is due to the limited amount of time between flights.

If your baggage does not arrive when you do, immediately notify a representative of the airline. Most airlines have a representative located in the baggage claim area. When the delayed luggage arrives at your destination airport, the airline will usually send it to where you are staying. There should be no charge for this service.

Note: Limits of liability for lost or damaged baggage is not great, so if you can't afford to loose it, don't check it.
Limits:
For flights wholly between U.S. points - $1250 per passenger, not per bag. For most International flights - $9.07 per lb. Weight of baggage at check-in will determine value, e.g., 50 lb. = $453.50. Excess valuation may not be declared on certain valuable, fragile or perishable articles.
Remember to place only your *last name* inside and outside of your luggage. *Do not put your address and phone number on or in the luggage.*

4

Checking In

If you have been issued your ticket and boarding pass by your travel agent, or if you received them from your airline by mail, you may proceed directly to the boarding gate. If you don't have a boarding pass you may obtain it at the gate. Many airlines no longer allow for boarding passes to be issued prior to your arrival at the airport. Your travel agent will inform you of this policy. **There is no need to stop at the ticket counter unless you must change your original ticket.** If you have to change your return ticket this may be done at the return airport's ticket counter. Electronic ticketed passengers may proceed directly to the gate, present a photo ID, and the gate agent will issue a boarding pass. On your return flight proceed in the same manner as above.

Be alert for a gate change, the one you check in at may not be the one you depart from.

Gate change announcements are generally NOT broadcast in restaurants, shops and airline clubs.

The airline may cancel your reservation and seat assignment if you don't present yourself at the boarding gate within a set time before scheduled departure, usually 10 or 15 minutes. Check with your travel agent or airline for departure requirements.

NOTE: Remember, if cancellation occurs, the airline has probably canceled your entire itinerary.

Departure delays can occur and are caused by several situations. Inclement weather not just at your departure airport, but at previous airports from where your flight is arriving, can affect your departure time. Remember each flight doesn't have its own aircraft. The airplane you will be boarding may have been on several flights that day, and may have been subjected to delays.

If your schedule permits, you can usually avoid delays by taking an early A.M. flight, since chances are the aircraft and the flight crew spent the night there.

Mechanical problems that affect the safety and comfort of the passengers and crew will be addressed prior to departure. Airplanes consist of thousands of moving parts and are subject to mechanical failures. Usually they can be repaired with little delay, depending on the severity and availability of parts.

When a gate agent announces a delay, they are relaying information from flight dispatchers and mechanics. The announcement of a new departure time, referred to as an estimated time of departure (E.T.D.), may be changed several times depending on the extent of the repair and the availability of parts and mechanics. All airports do not stock parts or have mechanics available. A flight may be canceled, at which time the airline will try to accommodate the passengers on the next available flight or on another airline. This sometimes requires routing you through other cities.

I know this can be frustrating, but please don't take your frustrations out on the gate agents. They didn't cause the problem, and they will do everything in their power to help you get to your destination.

When your flight is canceled, agents at the airport will assist you in rescheduling your flight. This can be time consuming. And annoying. Usually the number of employees available to assist you is limited, so it is wise to telephone your travel agent or airline as soon as possible and have an agent reschedule you. (See Chapter Twenty-five, Airline Telephone Numbers) They will have all the information available to them and will reschedule you without the confusion that occurs at the airport when there's a mass exodus off the aircraft and a near mob scene at the gate. Even at that, however, you still may have to go to the ticket counter to have your ticket reissued.

A canceled flight is stressful for the average traveler, so remember, as soon as you know of the cancellation you should:

♦   Listen to the announcement at the gate, if there is one.

♦   If they state that all passengers will be accommodated on the next flight, (may be on another airline), note the flight number, airline, time of departure and gate number if available.

♦   Telephone your travel agent or airline immediately. They will have firsthand knowledge of the cancellation and may have already protected you by having made a reservation for you on another flight.

♦   Ask if you must go to the ticket counter to have your ticket reissued. If yes, proceed there immediately to avoid long delays by fellow passengers.

♦ If you have an electronic ticketing boarding pass and reservation, you will be reissued
a boarding pass on your new flight at the gate.

Remember: if you are taking a late departure
and your flight cancels, there may not be any flights
available for the remainder of the day. To avoid this
problem, it is always advisable to leave as early as
possible to allow for back-up flights.

Also, remember that when your flight cancels
you will not be automatically rescheduled on the next
flight. There must be seats available on the flight. You
will not displace passengers that hold a reservation
on the flight. **Again, The Earlier The Flight The
Better.**

Flight Delays

There may come a time when you arrive at the
gate to find there's a mechanical problem with the aircraft causing a delay, even though the aircraft has
been parked at the gate for some time. The only concern you should have is what effect this delay will have
on your schedule. All too often passengers are concerned as to their safety on the aircraft. This concern
can remain with a passenger throughout the flight
causing alarm and doubt. Airline personnel, service
employees and flight crews often do not address these

concerns, mainly because the delays are usually of a technical nature. I've seen flights delayed while ground personnel frantically tried to locate a coffee-pot to replace a leaking one. If you're concerned about a delay, feel free to ask the pilot for an explanation. Flight crews welcome your inquiries and will do everything to make your flight comfortable and worry free. They are proud of their profession and take exceptional pride in giving passengers a safe and enjoyable flight.

I have heard passengers on canceled flights complain that the reason for the cancellation was the flight didn't have enough passengers. In my thirty years with the airlines I've never seen this occur. Not once. Cancelling flights because of too few passengers would create an adverse domino effect on the airlines' daily scheduling as each aircraft is scheduled for several flights each day. If one flight cancels, others would be forced to cancel as well. Running a business that way makes no bottom-line sense.

However, I did hear of a cancellation that caused a public relations nightmare. A large discount airline recently called a flight back to Dallas after it departed for Phoenix, deplaned the passengers, canceled the flight and inconvenienced passengers, some who missed their connections and had to spend the night at a hotel. It seems that a major league sports team was to depart Dallas on a charter flight to California, but their aircraft had a problem. I bet you can figure out what happened next. You got it, they put the ball team on the passengers' airplane. Because of the ensuing publicity, I don't think they will ever do that again.

There are other delays, too.

Crew delays: It used to make my day when I'd hear a airline agent announce to passengers, "This flight will be delayed because the pilots need their beauty sleep." Sure, blame the pilots. A flight may be delayed because the crew who is scheduled to fly your aircraft is delayed on an inbound flight, or the crew arrived late the previous evening and did not have the required rest hours as dictated by the Federal Aviation Administration. Airlines do not have crews available at every airport they serve, (crew bases).

Over-booked flights: Most flights are intentionally over-booked, selling more seats than are available. Airlines must protect themselves from loss revenue due to passenger no-shows (a passenger who makes a reservation and fails to show up for a flight). If you are denied boarding due to an over sale, the airline will ask for volunteers to stay behind and take a later flight, and may offer monetary and or free travel vouchers for their inconvenience. If you are not in a hurry to get to your destination, this offer can be lucrative since many airlines offer free round-trip transportation to any city they serve in the continental United States.

All right. So what happens when we're all checked in but have nowhere to go? What do we do until departure time? Well, we can

♦   Find a quiet area and read a good book.
♦   Locate a restaurant and have something to eat. Because of the delay it's possible no meals will be served once airborne.
♦   Enjoy your favorite beverage at a cocktail lounge while watching TV.
♦   Locate an airline club if you are a member. This is an excellent way to await your flight departure and most of the above is usually available at no or minimal charge.
♦   Browse through the gift shops, or do something that is educational and will enhance your knowledge of flying.

If you have a really long time to wait before your departure, take a tour of the air traffic control tower. Air traffic control towers are operated by highly skilled professionals of the Federal Aviation Administration and take great pride in showing their skills to the traveling public. Most towers are located in or close to airline terminals. Access must be approved by the tower chief (manager), who can be contacted by telephone (numbers available at airline service counters), during normal weekday business hours.

Tower personnel will make every effort to accommodate you if staffing and air traffic volume allows a tour with a minimum of distraction. Directing air traffic is a precise and demanding job requiring the utmost in concentration, and safety is paramount. I highly recommend this enlightening tour. If your travel is on a weekend and staffing permits, the controllers will make every effort to accommodate you.

5

Security

I remember the days of flying with the cockpit door open and inviting the passengers up front to see the workings of the cockpit crew. Then someone thought of a novel way to get to Cuba. And then came the threat of terrorism.

Travel on U.S. airlines is the safest in the world. Mutual cooperation between the airlines and the Federal Government has put in place an excellent security system to protect the traveling public. Unfortunately, besides being inconvenient, airport security has become increasingly costly, and this added expense is reflected in the cost of your ticket.

When making your reservation ask what identification will be required upon check-in at the airport.

These requirements do change so call your travel agent or airline prior to your flight. Most airlines have a voice recording addressing this issue on their reservation telephone line. Currently, unless you are under 18, you must have one photo ID issued by a Government agency, for example, a Drivers License, Passport, etc. Because of increased security, it is recommended that you allow one-hour check-in time for domestic and two hours for international travel. Distances in airports from arriving domestic flights to international departure flights are generally great. Check-in times are longer due to security and long lines at ticket counters. Some airlines are closing out flights 30 minutes prior to departure (Completed Boarding).

In airports such as Miami with flights to the Caribbean and South America it takes ages to process the luggage. Many passengers take numerous items purchased in the U.S. with them. Passengers with carry-on bags may be subject to delays, so the less you carry the sooner you will clear security.

Metal Detectors:

Remove all metal items from your pockets incluing metal adorned belts, bracelets, coins, keys, chains, etc. and deposit them in the containers provided at security. This allows you an uneventful passage through the metal detectors. Inform the security personnel if you have a surgical implant such as a pacemaker, metal rod, metal plate, etc. as those implants will activate the metal detector's alarm.

If you carry a camera and film, or a lap top personal computer, I recommend that you don't allow these items to go through the x-ray or metal detectors. Have the security personnel inspect these items by hand. Better safe than sorry.

NOTE: If traveling with a companion, allow them to clear security first so he or she can keep watch of your personal belongings as they clear the x-ray machine.

Thieves normally operate in pairs. One will clear security, and the other will cause a delay at the metal detector, preventing you from clearing the metal detector and allowing for the theft of your belongings. Stay alert. Keep your personal items in sight and close to you at all times.

WARNING

You must never check or attempt to carry on an aircraft explosive material of any kind or any type of weapon, real or fake, loaded or not, even if you are licensed to carry it.

At no time should you make a verbal comment about weapons, bombs or hijackings in jest.

Infractions of any of the above will subject you to immediate arrest.

This is extremely important. Do not violate this rule.

6

Boarding Your Flight

When the aircraft is ready to board, the gate agent will first accommodate passengers traveling with children and passengers requiring assistance, such as those in wheel chairs and other preboards. They will then begin boarding by row assignment, usually from the rear of the aircraft to the front. This allows passengers easy access to their seats and overhead storage compartments without walking around passengers in the aisle.

If you're carrying hanging bags, place these in the coat closets on the way to your seat. Carry-on luggage should be placed in the overhead compartments.

Remember that overhead storage compartments were designed for small carry-on bags and wearing apparel, not large pieces of luggage. Heavy bags placed in the overhead compartments have caused serious injuries when an aircraft was involved in an accident.

Several years ago a DC-9 jet overshot a landing, and wound up in a ditch at the end of the runway. Most of those injured suffered head and neck injuries caused by the collapse of the overhead storage compartments.

Always check large heavy bags as well as large hanging bags.

Numbers and letters identify seats. Numbers designate aisles and letters designate seats. Higher numbers are usually in the rear, lower ones in the front. The rows and seats are identified by number and letter markings located on the overhead storage compartment, or on the window seat wall.

Once seated, fasten your seat belt snugly around your lap. Move about the cabin only when attending to personal needs. If the Captain turns the seat belt sign off, this indicates that to the best of his knowledge, no turbulence is to be encountered. But this is no guarantee that the aircraft will *not* encounter severe turbulance associated with clear cloudless skies. Passengers have been severely injured in these encounters.

Remember you must keep the seat belt on at all times while seated. At press time many airlines are making this mandatory.

Review the safety and passenger comfort information provided by the airline, which is usually located in the seat back pocket. Safety items include locating and using emergency exits, use of life vests, emergency landings and information about unusual events (such as loss of cabin pressure). Since your safety depends on this information, Read it.

Interested in passenger comfort items, air condition outlets, music and video selections, telephone, fax and computer terminal information? All these are explained in the information section of the in-flight magazine provided by the airline located in the seat back pocket. (But you should be aware that these items may not be available on all flights.)

NOTE: Advise your travel agent or airline reservations agent when selecting a seat if you are traveling with a minor under 15 years of age. Federal Law forbids minors to sit in seats that are located in rows that have access to emergency exits.

I recently witnessed a 15-minute departure delay when a parent traveling with a minor refused to relocate to a non-exit aisle. The Captain was summoned and he informed the passenger of impending arrest by airport police for interfering with the duties of a flight crew. Needless to say, they relocated to another seat.

Large framed passengers, for extra comfort and convenience, should request, **in advance,** seats that are located in emergency exit rows because these usually offer additional leg room. These seats will be assigned at the boarding gate after verifying that the passenger is physically capable of operating the exit.

Arrive at the gate as early as possible for these seat assignments.

If you require a wheel chair at your destination, be sure and remind the flight attendant of your needs so one will be available at the arrival gate.

7

Taxiing to the Runway for Take-Off

When the passengers have been boarded and the aircraft serviced, the flight attendants will close the cabin doors and prepare the aircraft and passengers for departure. At most airports the aircraft will be pushed back from the gate by a vehicle (tug), which is attached to the front landing gear (nose wheel). During push back the pilots will start the engines. This requires turning off the air-conditioning, allowing for a faster and more efficient engine start by diverting the airflow to the engine starting system. You may notice that the air-conditioning outlets above your seat stop functioning, and passengers reaching for the outlets attempting to reinstate the airflow to no avail. (But you won't do that, will you? You'll know why they're not working.)

Once the engines have been started the pilot will direct the conditioned air to the passenger cabin. If your aircraft is parked in the close proximity of another aircraft you may notice the odor of its exhaust coming into the cabin through your aircraft's air-conditioning. Pilots will usually position the aircraft to avoid this, but at some congested airports this may be unavoidable.

The pilot may not start all the engines until the flight has been cleared for takeoff, and may shut down the engines if the flight will be experiencing a lengthy air traffic delay. Air traffic control (ATC) might delay the flight at the gate or direct the aircraft to a parking area if they foresee a delay en route due to weather or air traffic congestion at the arrival airport. This is known as Flow Control.

When the flight is released by ATC for takeoff, the engines will be restarted and the aircraft will continue to taxi onto the runway. While taxiing, the flight attendants will brief you on matters concerning your safety and comfort.

Pay particular attention to this briefing. This information will help you to avoid injuries in the unlikely event of an emergency. You have a responsibility to you and your fellow passengers to thoroughly understand the emergency procedure information provided you by the airline.

Over the years I've witnessed passengers ignoring the pre-departure emergency briefing as if it didn't matter. **If you fly twice a year or twice a day pay attention to these briefings.** I still listen to the briefings **and** review the information card provided for me in the seat back pocket.

Recently three hijackers demanding to be flown to Australia commandeered an Ethiopian Boeing 767. The aircraft did not have sufficient fuel to accommodate their demands and the hijackers refused to allow the pilots to land the aircraft to refuel. The flight was forced to continue until its fuel was exhausted resulting in a water landing and the ensuing loss of several lives. A survivor testified that just prior to the aircraft making contact with the water one passenger inflated his life preserver, (which all passengers had put on in preparation for an emergency water landing), triggering a chain reaction by numerous other passengers. A very distinct loud popping sound is generated during life preserver inflation. This action was contrary to the instructions of the flight crew and the printed information provided by the airline on the emergency information card, namely,

Do Not Inflate The Life Preserver Until You Are Outside The Aircraft

The aircraft rapidly filled with water after breaking up during touchdown. Unfortunately, because the inflated life jackets restricted passengers' movement to the exits, many of those who inflated their life jackets *prior* to exiting drowned inside the cabin.

Again, pay attention to pre-departure emergency instructions and follow the flight crew's instructions. Your life depends on it.

What's that sound?

Passengers are subject to many sounds while on the aircraft and not knowing their origin often causes concern and alarm.

While taxiing the pilot will extend take-off flaps and slats, will set the air-conditioning and pressurization controls, the electrical generators, turn on the hydraulic pumps and turn off the auxiliary power unit (APU). If the aircraft has been parked for a long period of time, like overnight, you may notice that the aircraft is experiencing a bumpy taxi. This is caused by flat spots on the tires from being parked in one position for a long time and will disappear during taxi and takeoff.

8

Take-Off
and Climb

Now that you've been briefed, the engines
are purring, and the aircraft's been cleared onto the
runway for takeoff, sit back, relax and settle down to
enjoy your flight.

When takeoff clearance is received, the pilot
will be issued a heading and altitude to comply with.
The throttles will be advanced to takeoff power and
the aircraft will accelerate to takeoff speed. As the
aircraft accelerates you may hear a thumping noise
whose frequency increases with acceleration. This is
associated with the nose wheel tires rolling over the
runway center line lights, which are a series of re-
cessed lights in the center of the runway. To avoid
this sometimes-disturbing sound the pilot may steer
the aircraft slightly to the left or right of the

centerline. Just prior to lifting off the pilot will rotate the nose of the aircraft at a speed referred to as Vr, (velocity rotation). The plane will then lift off the runway at a speed slightly higher than Vr, referred to as V2 (Lift-off Speed).

Once the aircraft is airborne the pilot will retract the landing gear into the aircraft (wheel wells), causing possible vibration and accompanying noise. You may hear sounds of the hydraulic pumps, which provide pressure to the landing gear and the flap and slat systems. These sounds are normal. Don't be alarmed.

Next the pilot will retract the flaps on the rear of the wings and the slats on the front of the wings. This procedure will make sounds similar but not quite as noticeable as the landing gear retraction. I've always wondered on takeoff why they don't call the wheels the Takeoff Gear.

The pilot may make a series of heading and altitude changes as required by ATC. The latter would require engine power changes. If so, these would generate fluctuating engine sounds.

To avoid flying over noise sensitive areas such as housing developments, hospitals, etc., departing and arriving aircraft may make a series of heading and altitude changes with associated engine power changes, a procedure referred to as Noise Abatement.

This can require large heading and power changes. Once again, don't be alarmed. Noise abatement procedures are easily flown and are very safe.

Anyone who has flown out of Washington D.C.'s National Airport is aware of this procedure.

Once the pilots have accomplished the above, the aircraft will climb to its assigned altitude. This may require several altitude changes, in compliance with ATC. Each time your aircraft levels off in route to its cruising altitude, expect to hear engine power changes.

Just after liftoff and during climb the aircraft cabin will begin pressurizing for your comfort, and you may feel pressure changes in your ears. **Passengers easily adapt to ascending pressure changes.**

9

Cruise

Once the aircraft has reached its assigned cruising altitude the pilot may turn off the *Fasten Seat Belt* sign followed by an announcement that passengers are free to move about the cabin. But I suggest you do this only while attending to personal needs, lavatory, etc.

Note: While moving through the cabin make use of the seat backs and in the lavatory, the wall mounted handles.

Even though the seat belt sign has been turned off, this is no guarantee that the aircraft will not encounter severe turbulence. Keep your seat belt fastened while seated.

Occasionally your flight will encounter choppy or turbulent flight conditions and the pilot will climb or descend to a smoother altitude, if known. The pilot ascertains this by asking ATC or other flights in the area. In rare situations turbulence may be reported at all cruise altitudes. For jet aircraft, cruise altitudes are 18,000 feet and above. At these altitudes they are referred to as flight levels (FL), for example, 18000 ft = FL 180, − 35,000 ft = FL 350.

Altitude changes must be approved by ATC and sometimes that approval is delayed due to conflicting traffic, that is, aircraft above, below or crossing your path. These delays are rare and if encountered are minimal.

Sometimes you might notice a fluctuation in the volume of air coming from the overhead air-condition outlets. This is directly related to power changes made by the pilot since the air-condition compressors are an integral part of the power plant (engines). You may also hear the hydraulic pumps cycling on and off. This usually is a momentary condition.

Smoking is banned on all airlines in the United States. Learn to live with it.

DON'T EVER ATTEMPT TO SMOKE ON AN AIRPLANE.

Smoking on an airplane is a violation of Federal Law, and violators will be arrested. Passengers have attempted smoking in the lavatories not realizing there were several detection devices in and about this area, and were promptly arrested upon landing. There have been occasions where smokers caused fires in the lavatories by improperly disposing of lighted cigarettes and initiating emergency landings with subsequent injuries, some fatal.

When your flight reaches a comfortable cruising altitude the flight attendants will begin food and beverage service. Beverages, excluding alcohol, are usually complimentary, and are served first if a meal service is offered. Meal service has been somewhat curtailed since the advent of deregulation and discount fares. Airline competition has become intense and airlines are constantly seeking ways to reduce operating costs without compromising safety. Since meals cost the airlines hundreds of millions of dollars annually, not serving them has been one aspect of cost-cutting.

Today it's possible to cross the continental United States on a flight or series of flights lasting 10 or more hours, including ground connecting time, and be offered only a snack like peanuts or pretzels. If food is important to you, check with your travel agent or airline about the availability of meal service and plan accordingly, especially if departing during meal hours

Special meals, such as Asian, Asian vegetarian, baby, bland, chef salad, chicken, child, cold seafood, diabetic, fish, fruit/deli, fruit plate, gluten free, high fiber, high protein, Hindu, hot seafood, Japanese, Korean, kosher, lactose free, lacto-vegetarian, low calorie, low carbohydrate, low cholesterol, low fat, low protein, low purine, low sodium, low sugar, Muslim, non dairy, no salt, oriental, raw vegetarian, seafood, soft diet, sulfite free, vegetarian, vegetarian non dairy, are available on most airlines and must be ordered in advance, usually when making your reservation. Have your travel agent check to see what special meals are offered on your flight. Reconfirm your special meal order 24 hours in advance of your flight, and when boarding your flight notify the gate agent and flight attendant of your meal request.

NOTE: Diabetics should carry a supply of foods with them in case of delays, etc.

To make a passenger's flight comfortable and enjoyable airlines have invested millions of dollars on entertainment centers located at your seat. You can select from a menu consisting of full-length feature films, information channels, telephones, facsimile, computer on-line service and various selections of music and entertainment channels. Information on this may be found in the in-flight magazine, located in your seat back pocket. Remember though that some aircraft may not be equipped with in-flight entertainment.

10

Descent and Landing

Prior to the aircraft's descent the flight attendants will collect all food and beverage service items. Occasionally, due to the length of a flight, the collection process may continue into the descent. At this time make certain your seat belt is securely fastened. When the pilot receives the descent clearance, it will usually consist of several altitude and heading changes, with associated reductions and increases of engine power.

Depending on the volume of arrivals, departures, and weather conditions at your destination airport, you might encounter in flight delays. During adverse landing conditions, rain, sleet, snow, fog or gusty surface winds, air traffic controllers may increase the horizontal separation between landing aircraft to allow for a greater margin of safety.

This could be required due to the increased landing distances on wet runways and additional time required to exit the runway.

Occasionally the aircraft will not be able to land because of ceiling and visibility requirements and will begin a holding pattern rather than fly to another destination. With new automatic landing systems installed in today's modern jet aircraft it's a rare occasion when a flight has to proceed to an alternate airport. A flight will hold as long as safety is not compromised.

When an aircraft is released for flight, the pilots and dispatchers have agreed as to the amount of fuel required for a safe flight. Federal Regulations require that a flight must have sufficient fuel to arrive at its destination, execute a missed approach, continue to the alternate airport and execute an approach and landing. They must also have a 45-minute reserve, as well as a specified amount of holding fuel.

Fuel quantity gauges are calibrated to indicate the amount of fuel in pounds instead of gallons. One gallon of jet fuel equals 6.7 lb.

The following is an explanation of how fuel consumption is calculated.

Flight Plan for Fuel Consumption

From La Guardia Airport to Tampa, Florida	12,000 lb.	1791 gal.
From Tampa to Orlando, Alternate	3,000 lb.	447 gal.
Two Approaches	600 lb.	89 gal.
Forty-five Minute Reserve	4,500 lb.	671 gal.
Total Required Fuel	20,100 lb.	3000 gal.
Holding Fuel	5,000 lb.	746 gal.
Total Dispatch Fuel	25,100 lb.	3746 gal.

These figures are based on a two hour flight in a twin engine jet, for example, a DC-9, with an average fuel burn (consumption) of 6000 lb. per hour.

NOTE: It is a Federal requirement that the 45-minute reserve fuel is to be used only in emergency situations.

The amount of holding fuel is determined by several factors: forecasted weather conditions at the destination airport, air traffic delays and the allowable landing weight of the aircraft at its destination. What do we mean by allowable landing weight?

Let's refer to the above example.

At La Guardia Airport the take-off weight was 110,000 lb. (aircraft empty weight + fuel + passengers + baggage + cargo + supplies)

The maximum allowable landing weight at Tampa is 98,000 lb.

The flight plan shows a fuel consumption of 12,000 lb. from New York to Tampa with one approach at Tampa, 300 lb., for a total fuel burn of 12,300 lb.

Take-off weight	110,000 lb.
Fuel burn	- 12,300 lb.
Landing weight at Tampa	= 97,700 lb.
Maximum landing weight at Tampa	98,000 lb.

If the aircraft was dispatched with 25,100 lb. of fuel, according to the above figures it could have added an additional 300 lb. of holding fuel. Subtracting the fuel burn of 12,300 lb. from the Take-off weight equals an actual landing weight of 97,700 lb. Since the maximum landing weight at Tampa is 98,000 lb. the difference would allow for an additional 300 lb. of holding fuel for a maximum holding fuel of 5,300 lb.

As previously discussed in Chapter Eight, pilots may be required to follow noise abatement procedures on approach and landing. These approaches may require steep turns, descents and large adjustments to engine power settings. These procedures are easily followed by the pilot and are very safe.

During approach and landing you will hear numerous sounds as the pilot prepares the aircraft for landing. To slow the aircraft to landing speed and maintain aerodynamic lift the pilot will extend trailing edge flaps, rear of wing, and leading edge slats, front of wing. This is accomplished in several sequenced steps. Flaps are extended by degrees, 1-5-10-15-25-30-40-50. (These degrees vary depending on the make and model of the aircraft.) Slats usually extend in sequence with the flaps, but again depending on the model may be positioned to their full extent in one motion.

You'll hear sounds and experience vibrations associated with the selection of the landing gear to the down and locked position in preparation for landing. At this time again check to see that your seat belt is fastened.

As the aircraft touches down on the runway you'll notice the deployment of devices on the top of the wing to a near vertical position. These are ground spoilers and their function is simply to spoil the aerodynamic lift of the wing. This reduces the flying ability of the wing allowing for the full weight of the aircraft to rest on the runway, enhancing the braking action, allowing for a shorter landing distance. Moments after ground spoiler deployment the pilot will apply reverse thrust to assist the stopping process.

Contrary to belief, the engines **do not** reverse their motion but continue to develop forward thrust. Devices on the rear of the engines deflect the thrust forward.

The combination of ground spoilers, reverse thrust and brakes are a very effective means of stopping the aircraft. Engine reversal sounds will be quite noticeable.

When the aircraft's forward speed has been slowed sufficiently to allow a safe exit from the runway, the pilot will turn the aircraft using a steering device that controls the movement of the nose wheel. Two types of runway exit taxiways are available, a 90 degree and a high speed. Exiting on to a 90-degree taxiway requires a slow speed and a sharp 90-degree turn while a high-speed taxiway allows for a faster, gentler exit.

NOTE: While jet transports are designed to stop using only brakes, the additional use of ground spoilers and reverse thrust enhances the stopping efficiency.

BUT WHAT ABOUT THOSE TIMES YOU CAN'T LAND FOR AWHILE. WHAT'S GOING ON THEN?

Flying a racetrack pattern at a geographic point (fix), is the most common way of holding a flight that can't land. ATC (air traffic control) will assign a specific altitude, airspeed and the direction of turns. ATC will also issue the pilot an "expect further clearance" time, referred to as EFC, at which time the pilot will receive a clearance beyond the fix or receive an amended time to depart the fix. It is not unusual for a flight to depart a fix prior to its EFC time. If the expected delays are not lengthy, the flight may be directed to execute one or more turns (360s) or may reduce its speed to allow greater in trail spacing. There's nothing to worry about. You'll land eventually. And safely. Just remember that patience is a virtue.

11

Taxiing to Jetway / Gate for Deplaning

Once the aircraft has exited the runway the pilot will taxi the aircraft to its assigned gate for passenger deplaning. Airlines assign gates to flights according to their schedule arrival and departure times. On arrival, a flight may experience a "gate delay" if a departure flight is experiencing a delay or the arrival flight has arrived at the gate earlier than scheduled. This is most frequent at congested airports where scheduled gate times between departures and arrivals may be just minutes.

While holding for a gate, you might notice un-occupied gates and wonder why your flight hasn't taxied to one of them. *Because gate agents and passengers are waiting to board your aircraft at the assigned gate.* They'd have to relocate, and there'd be more delays and passenger confusion. This procedure would also cause a snowballing delay effect on other flights. If an unoccupied gate can be utilized to accommodate your flight without causing additional delays and confusion, the airline will do so.

At most airports passengers will deplane through jetways. In some instances, where jetways are not available or not serviceable, they'll deplane onto the ramp. Jetways allow you to enter the terminal with little or no exposure to weather conditions, whereas deplaning onto the ramp may subject you to inclement weather conditions.

While taxiing to the parking area, for you and your fellow passenger's safety, don't attempt to remove your seat belt and stand until you've been instructed to by a crew member. Your aircraft may make several complete stops before reaching the deplaning gate, so wait for the signal from the crew. You may have just traveled thousands of miles in a few hours so why risk injury by trying to deplane first. An orderly deplaning process (boarding process in reverse) is just that: orderly. And requires little time, as well. Contrast that with a hundred or so passengers clogging the aisle reaching for personal effects in the overhead compartments. Wait it out. You'll have less aggravation.

When you're ready to leave, be certain you've removed any items of yours from the overhead compartment and the coat closet.

If you'd like to comment about your flight to the cockpit crew, do so prior to deplaning. They'd be happy to answer your questions and do appreciate your comments.

NOTE: If your flight has passengers whose connections are awaiting their arrival, the flight attendant may request that they deplane first. Be considerate of their needs and allow them unrestricted access in the aisle so they can exit quickly.

12

Connecting Flights

Once inside the terminal, information pertaining to ones connecting flight may be obtained from TV monitors located in the boarding area. TV monitors display gate assignments, arrivals and departure times, both scheduled and actual. You can also request assistance from airline passenger service representatives located in the gate area.

A particular airline flight will usually arrive and depart from the same terminal, making connections relatively easy. In rare cases an airline may utilize more than one terminal to accommodate a great number of flights within a short period of time.

Verify that your connecting flight is on the same airline as your arrival.

If your connecting flight is on a different airline, request directions to the departure gate.

If your inbound flight is delayed, advise an airline representative in the gate area so you can be assisted in making your connection. **Be aware that you may be required to go through security again if your connecting flight is in a different boarding area.**

Be prepared for long walks between gates when making connections in some of the larger airline terminals. Most airlines offer a free shuttle service between gates, so if the distance is lengthy and you don't feel physically capable of walking great distances, or if your connecting time is short, ask a gate agent or passenger service representative for assistance.

In the unlikely event you miss your connecting flight the airline will do what it can to get you to your destination as soon as possible. Many passengers are under the false impression that once their original flight cancels, or if they miss their connecting flight due to a reason beyond their control, that the airline will put them on the next scheduled flight. Not necessarily so: You'll be accommodated on the **first available flight** — one that has available seats.

If you started your trip late in the day and miss your connection there is a remote possibility that no other flights will be available that evening. You may have to spend the night at your connecting city. Be prepared for this possibility.

As stated in Chapter One, **when possible, take a non-stop flight to avoid being inconvenienced**.

Non-Stop = one flight = no stops.

13

Claiming Luggage

If you are arriving on an international flight be prepared to proceed to customs and immigration. Usually your flight attendant will distribute entry forms before landing that must be completed prior to clearing customs in the international arrival area. Your luggage will be claimed in this area and presented for inspection.

Domestic passengers may proceed directly to baggage claim. Follow posted directions to the baggage claim area allowing some time for your luggage to arrive.

Because some baggage claim areas are located a great distance from where you deplane, you may experience a delay of the arrival of your luggage. Delays can be lengthy depending on the number of flights being serviced and weather conditions on the ramp. Luggage handlers are not permitted on the ramp during storms that produce lightning.

When the luggage arrives in the claim area have your claim checks readily available for positive identification since many bags look alike. Identifying your luggage can be relatively simple if you put a readily identifiable personal mark on your luggage. Use colored ribbon, tape or a personalized nametag. For safety's sake, do not include your address or phone number.

Skycaps are available in the baggage area to retrieve and carry your bags to your transportation. Just as with curbside check-in, the customary gratuity is $1.00 per bag.

Prior to leaving the claim area you should examine your luggage for damage and or pilfering. Baggage service representatives are located in the claim area to handle irregularities. The airline representative will provide you with information regarding lost or damaged luggage and limits of liability.

Do not leave the airport before informing an agent of the loss or damage, and receiving a receipt for your property.

14

Transportation from the Airport

If you are to be transported from the airport in a private vehicle, have the driver park in the closest parking area and meet you at the arrival area or baggage claim. Remind the driver to telephone the airline prior to leaving for the airport. and verify your flight's arrival time. Many airports will not allow anyone to park and wait at the terminal baggage claim area, but will allow vehicles to park if the passenger has already retrieved his or her luggage and is ready for immediate pick up.

Parking in a designated area will avoid congestion in the baggage claim area.

Other means of transportation are rental cars, taxis, airport limos and public transportation. (See Chapter Two for advantages and disadvantages)

Rental car companies are readily available in most airline baggage claim areas and some within a short distance from the airport. Reservations are recommended.

15

Food and Beverage Service

Deregulation of the airlines has allowed for greater competition with the addition of many new no frill discount airlines. To compete in today's marketplace airlines must reduce their overall operating expenses. This can be accomplished in many ways including but not limited to lower than standard industry wages, maintenance subcontracting, and a reduction of, if not total elimination of, food and beverage service.

It is entirely possible for a passenger to board an early morning flight from the East Coast making one or more connections to the West Coast, a trip of possibly eight or more flying hours and many more hours at airports, encompassing the breakfast, lunch and dinner periods, without being offered a meal.

In very competitive markets you may receive meals with a total disregard for regular meal hours. The longer a non-stop flight, the better the chances are that you'll receive a meal. Again, check with your travel agent about the availability of meal service. If in doubt, allow extra time to eat at the airport. To be safe (and not hungry) I highly recommend brown bagging sandwiches and snacks on most flights today. Even if you are served food it is usually high in fat and sodium content or is barely edible. If you're told a snack will be served, expect anything from a sandwich to a bag of peanuts.

Meals and snacks vary greatly according to the class of reservation you hold — First, Business, or Economy. The amount of time you have to enjoy your meal depends on the length of the flight and where you sit in the cabin. A rule of thumb, the further forward you sit, the better chance of being served first. (See Chapter Twenty-seven for seating arrangements) Note that this rule applies primarily to Economy Class.

NOTE: See Chapter Nine for information on ordering special meals.

16

Unusual Events

Prior to takeoff your flight attendants will brief the passengers on certain emergency procedures. You should be aware that certain procedures associated with a particular unusual in-flight event, such as loss of cabin pressure, are not fully explained. If you happen to be involved in a loss of cabin pressure, a rare event, follow the procedures that were demonstrated prior to take off. Immediately reach for an oxygen mask and place it over your nose and mouth and breathe normally. Since this procedure is not considered part of a normal uneventful flight, it's not abnormal for you to show concern and alarm.

All modern airline transports are pressurized for passenger comfort. Rarely does the pressurization system not function. You could fly in an unpressurized cabin at 10,000 feet or below without any adverse effects from lack of oxygen. The higher an aircraft flies, the less the content of oxygen in the air. Modern jetliners cruise at 20,000 feet or higher where the oxygen content of the outside air is nil.

In the unlikely event of the loss of cabin pressure the pilot will prepare the aircraft for a descent to a lower altitude where you can breathe normally without the use of the oxygen mask. The pilots will immediately put their oxygen masks on and if they cannot regain control of the pressurization, they will begin the descent to a lower altitude. You'll notice that the engine sounds diminish as the power is retarded to idle.

If sitting in view of the wings, you would see the in-flight spoilers on the top of the wings raise to a near vertical position with associated rumbling sounds, and the pilot will descend quite rapidly to a lower altitude. The descent usually requires **a steep pitch down attitude,** which could be alarming. The process of establishing the aircraft in the descent — idle power, in-flight spoilers extended, pitching the aircraft into a steep descent — requires very little time, perhaps just a few seconds. Remember this is an unusual in-flight event requiring immediate pilot action. Don't be overly alarmed as the pilots have trained and practiced this procedure numerous times in the aircraft and simulator.

When the aircraft reaches its lower altitude the pilot will bring the aircraft back to level flight. You'll hear the increase in engine power, the pilot will stow the flight spoilers to their normal position, and you'll be advised to remove your mask. Depending on the proximity to the destination airport, the pilot may continue or elect to land at the nearest suitable airport. There the aircraft will be serviced so it can continue to its destination.

These oxygen masks do not supply 100% pure oxygen, but a mixture of cabin air and pure oxygen. Therefore, in the event of smoke in the cabin it is recommended you DO NOT use your oxygen mask since you'd be breathing smoke through it.

If you must evacuate the aircraft using emergency exits, be aware of the following:

Emergency windows are bulky, cumbersome, and very heavy. If you choose to sit at an emergency window, make certain you are physically capable of handling the important task of opening, removing, and stowing the window.

If the cabin is tilted to the side, expect the exit to fall in toward you if it is on the high side.

If you're not physically capable of this emergency procedure don't sit at the emergency exit. Your life and others depend on the ability of the individual at the emergency exit to comply with the emergency instructions. Above all listen to the flight crew. They are trained and capable of handling emergencies.

IMPORTANT- Read the emergency information prior to leaving the gate and pay strict attention to the flight crew's emergency briefings.

AGAIN, READ AND LISTEN TO THESE PROCEDURES. FOLLOW YOUR FLIGHT CREW'S INSTRUCTIONS.

Many emergency evacuations are of a precautionary nature. Unfortunately, some passengers are injured when they exit an aircraft under these circumstances.

To prevent injuries, or keep them to a minimum, remember:

♦ Some exits may not be useable due to conditions outside the aircraft such as fire, structural damage, etc.[*Follow the directions of the flight crew*].

♦ If traveling with children, ask your fellow passengers to assist you.

♦ Proceed [*without delay*] to the nearest exit or to the exits [*as directed by the flight crew*].

♦ Exercise caution when evacuating the aircraft. The distance between the exits and the surface can be great depending on the model of the aircraft.

Don't waste precious time retrieving your purse, coat and carry-on luggage. These are not as important as your life.
LEAVE THEM ON THE PLANE

"Ladies and gentlemen, this is your captain speaking. We have a slight problem and are returning to the airport. We will be landing in a few minutes, and will keep you informed on the status of our flight. And by the way, we will have to dump fuel prior to landing."

They're going to do what ?

Not to worry; this is an easy one to explain.

Fuel jettisoning, although safe, is a sight you may find disquieting. When fuel must be dumped, the fuel valves are positioned to allow the fuel to flow from the fuel tanks to the fuel jettisoning ports, which are usually located at the rear outboard section of the wing tips. When fuel hits the atmosphere it vaporizes, appearing similar to a jet contrail. If you're unaware of this procedure, the vapor trail you see streaning from the wing tips might spell disaster in your mind.

Rest assured, such is not the case. Jettisoning fuel is not uncommon.

Here's why: Let's say a particular aircraft is allowed to take off weighing 150,000 pounds, calculated on the basis it will use 25,000 pounds of fuel by the time of arrival at its destination, which places it well within its maximum landing weight of 130,000 pounds. But what if the aircraft has a in-flight problem and has to return to the airport before burning much fuel? Now the aircraft will exceed its maximum landing weight. So the captain makes the decision to dump 'x' number of pounds of fuel prior to landing to bring the aircraft within that maximum landing weight allowance of 130,000 pounds.

See, nothing to it. For you, the passenger, it's all a matter of knowing What's Going On.

17

Commuter Airlines

Commuter airlines are wholly owned and operated by the airline or are independent and privately owned and operated. They fill a void in the large airlines' route structure by offering frequent service to many airports not serviced by the parent airline.

The capacity of the commuter aircraft varies by the demand of the market place. Commuter aircraft seat from four or five passengers to as many as a hundred or more. They may be jet powered, propjet, or piston engine propeller aircraft. Flight attendants, food and beverage service and lavatories will be provided for your comfort and safety depending on the aircraft model seating capacity. Passengers may board through a jetway or via the ramp. Most commuter airplanes board and deplane on the ramp. Generally speaking, the smaller the aircraft, the less comfort items.

In the past year the safety issue has surfaced due to a few commuter aircraft accidents. Some commuter airlines operated under different standards than the larger airlines. (Pilot flight and on-duty time limitations.) The Federal Aviation Administration recently addressed these issues and has brought the commuter airlines in compliance with the industry.

Commuter pilot training is rigorous, demanding and exceeds the standards set by the FAA.

During my career I've flown on hundreds of commuter flights and not once did I witness a substandard operation.

I've had the pleasure to train and fly with pilots from commuter airlines as they moved up to what we refer to as the main line, the larger parent airline.

There is a good possibility that one, if not both of your pilots flying your next flight on a major airline flew at one time for a commuter.

18

Understanding Airfares

Most major airlines offer several options in ticket pricing. They may offer several prices for the same flight and date. These prices could vary several hundreds of dollars. Since the advent of the so-called "air wars," airlines change fares almost on an hourly basis. Do your homework. Spend the time to inquire about these fares. Of course, the easiest and most convenient way to do this is through your travel agent.

Ask your travel agent to check for the lowest fare available when making your reservation and be sure and check with him or her a day or so before your flight to see if anything lower is offered. If you make a reservation for a one way flight, that is, no return flight, have your travel agent check if a round trip fare is available at a lower fare. Believe it or not, it's sometimes cheaper to buy a round trip ticket than a one way, even if you decide to discard the return portion.

A fare frenzy often occurs when one airline advertises a sale. Competing airlines — those that fly the same routes — will generally match or beat the advertised prices. You'll probably have a lengthy wait on the telephone trying to reach an airline reservation agent. What to do?

Call your travel agent!
They can access the airlines reservation
system directly.

Remember that sale prices generally are not for all seats on all flights. Sometimes as few as 10% of a flight may be offered at a sale price.

For your protection, purchase your ticket with a credit card in case of a flight stoppage due to the airline ceasing operations. This is especially important if it is a relatively new airline that has been experiencing financial problems.

19

Unaccompanied Minor Children

Due to the ever-increasing number of separations and divorces the airlines find themselves accommodating thousands of unaccompanied minor children each week. These parents who have relocated to different geographic areas and have specific visitation rights will find the airlines cooperative and understanding of a parent's concern for their children's safety and comfort.

Following are specific guidelines pertaining to children traveling alone such as age, time of day to travel, non-stop, through-flight, connecting flights, identification requirements, and service fees.

Age requirements, (most airlines) **No one under 5 years of age.**

Ages **5 through 8**, travel must be on a nonstop or a direct flight, with no change of aircraft;

Ages **9 through 11**, allowed to fly on connecting flights, (aircraft change allowed) but may be charged a service fee, ($30-$120, check with your travel agent).

Unaccompanied minor children are charged the same fare as adults. Your travel agent will obtain the most economical fare available. Certain restrictions may apply, such as length of stay, advance reservations, super savers, etc.

IMPORTANT NOTICE: What if the minor child is stranded at a connecting city or the authorized adult, for whatever reason, doesn't meet the child?

Listed below is a sample of rules and regulations governing the transportation of unaccompanied minors. **Call your travel agent to verify this information prior to departure. Fees are increasing.**

AIRTRAN

Minimum Age: 5 for non-stop flights; 8 for connecting flights. **Airport Supervision:** There is an Unaccompanied Minor Room, (private special service), at ATL (Atlanta) which is supplied with items to entertain unaccompanied minors. **Service Fee:** $25 when a connection is needed. **When a Child is stranded:** An airline supervisor stays with the child at all times.

AMERICA WEST

Minimum Age: 5 for nonstop or direct flights; 8 for connections. **Airport Supervision:** Escort to connecting flights. **Service fee:** $30 each way when connection is needed. **When a Child is Stranded:** If there are no friends or relatives in the area, children stay in a hotel; an airline employee stays in an adjoining room.

AMERICAN

Minimum Age: 5 for non-stops; 8 for connecting flights. **Airport Supervision:** Children are escorted between flights by an airline employee or designated contractor. **Service Fee:** $30 each way. **When a Child is Stranded:** Overnight policies vary according to the wishes of the child's parent or guardian, but non-siblings are not placed in the same hotel room.

CONTINENTAL

Minimum Age: 5 for nonstop or direct flights; 8 for connecting flight. **Airport Supervision:** For layovers of an hour or longer at CLE (Cleveland), IAH (Houston), and EWR (Newark), children are escorted to a Young Traveler's Club, stocked with munchies, beverages, and toys. **Service fees:** $30 each way for connecting flights. **When a Child is Stranded:** An airline employee stays with the child at all times.

DELTA

Minimum Age: 5 for non-stop and direct flights; 8 for connecting flights. **Airport Supervision:** Escort to connecting flights. Children's centers stocked with games, movies, books and snacks, are located in ATL (Atlanta), BOS (Boston), CVG (Cincinnati), DFW (Dallas Fort Worth), JFK (Kennedy, New York), LAX (Los Angeles), SLC (Salt Lake City), and TPA (Tampa). **Service fee:** $60 each way for connecting flights. **When a Child is Stranded:** There was no comment by a Delta spokesperson on specific guidelines but she did say the child's parent or guardian must approve them.

NORTHWEST

Minimum Age: 5 for both non-stop and connecting flights. **Airport Supervision:** Escort to connecting flights. Children's centers in DTW (Detroit) and MSP (Minneapolis Saint Paul) airports. **Service Fee:** $60 each way for connecting flights. **When a Child is Stranded:** After consultation with parent or guardian, the child is placed in a hotel room. A guard of the same sex is posted outside the room.

SOUTHWEST

Minimum Age: 5 for nonstop or direct flights; 12 for connecting flights. **Airport Supervision: NONE. Service Fee: NONE. When a Child is Stranded:** If possible, the child is returned to the original destination. If the authorized adults can't be contacted, the child will be turned over to a child welfare agency or the police.

TWA

Minimum Age: 5 for nonstop and connecting flights on TWA; 8 for connections on other carriers. **Airport Supervision:** Escort to connecting flights. Children's centers in JFK (Kennedy, New York), and STL (Saint Louis)are stocked with chalkboards,books, games, TV and snacks. **Service Fee:** $30 when a connection is required. **When a Child is Stranded:** A TWA employee is in the same room with the child at all times.

UNITED

Minimum Age: 5 for non-stops; 8 for connecting flights. **Airport Supervision:** Children with connecting flights are escorted between gates; at some airports children are taken to United Airlines special services center between flights. **Service Fee:** $30 each way. **When a Child is Stranded:** With parent or guardian's consent, children stay with a United employee in a hotel room or at the employee's home.

US AIRWAYS

Minimum Age: 5 for nonstop; 8 for connecting flights. **Airport Supervision:** Children are escorted to gates and supervised at all times. **Service**

Fee: $30 each way. **When a Child is Stranded:** The airline consults with the adults designated on the child's permission forms.

It is obvious from this list that requirements vary from airline to airline. Check these rules when making your reservation and prior to departure.

If the airline doesn't specify a charge for nonstop flights there usually isn't one.

Remember to make available for your travel agent the name, address, and phone number of the person meeting your child and give it to your travel agent when making the reservation. The person meeting the child will be required to show a picture ID, prior to the child being released by the airline representative.

To make your Child's Trip less stressful

♦ **THE EARLIER THE FLIGHT, THE BETTER.** Allows for alternate plans due to cancellation or delays. The aircraft and crew scheduled for early am flights usually have spent the evening at your departure airport, which means the flight didn't originate at another city. These flights are not normally subject to delays, since they're the first flights of the day.

♦ **NONSTOP FLIGHTS ARE A MUST IF AVAILABLE.** Peace of mind to realize your child will depart and arrive without making a stop and changing flights. If there is a more economical flight that requires an aircraft change or one that makes a stop, it is still in your child's best interest to go non stop. Pay the difference. Your travel agent will research these flights for you.

♦ CHANGE IN TIME ZONES. A parent must remember, **especially when travel is to be made from the west to east**, to consider the child's arrival time. In domestic travel there could be as much as a four-hour difference. Combine this with the flight time and your child could leave Los Angeles at 9am Pacific Time, and arrive in New York at 6pm local time, so it is important to arrange for an early departure for your child. **NON STOP if available**.

♦ MEDICAL RECORDS. You should obtain your child's records from his or her physician, and mail or fax a copy to the individual with whom the child will be staying. **Include a copy in the child's personal carry-on luggage.** Don't forget to advise the travel agent and the gate agent at the airport about these documents. Also include a notarized permission letter authorizing medical care and emergency treatment for your child while in transit. This document should be given to the airline representative at the airport and so noted. Do not forget to send one to the party meeting the child. Include in this document a statement of the child's general health and any reactions or allergies to medications.

♦ CHILDREN'S IDENTIFICATION. It is extremely important that an unaccompanied child has the proper identification with them. It should include the child's full name, address, social security number if available, blood type, a short history of any medical problems, any known allergies or reactions to medications, directions for taking current medications, child's physician's name and phone number, telephone numbers (home and work) of the parents or adults at the departure and arrival airports. Copies of this document should be distributed to the airline gate agent, the flight attendant, and the party meeting the child at the arrival airport. Retain a copy for yourself and put one in the child's pocket preferably, or in a small carry-on bag. Don't forget to tell your child where these documents are located. And place a name tag with phone number to the clothing the child will wear on the flight.

♦ FOOD SERVICE. If the airline offers meal service it is possible to special order a children's meal or if your child requires a special meal due to dietary or religious requirements these meals can be provided at no additional cost. **Special meals should be ordered at least 24 hours before flight departure.** Your travel agent or airline will make these arrangements for you. **Remind the gate agent and the flight attendant that you ordered a special meal.** It's advisable that your child have something to eat just prior to departure time so you don't have to depend on the child eating on the flight. Your child may be so enthralled with flying, watching an in-flight movie, listening to music, or reading a book that he or she won't eat. (If a movie is offered there usually is a charge for this service so make sure your child has sufficient funds.) Pack a supply of snacks in the small carry-on bag in case the meal was not satisfying or not offered.

♦ PROPER CLOTHING. If your child is traveling a distance be aware that the clothes worn at departure may not be suitable for the climate at the destination. **Pay special attention to the child's apparel if he or she is travel ing from warm to a cooler climate.** Make certain that suitable clothing is carried on board the aircraft so it will be readily available upon arrival.

Make a checklist of clothing that will be required upon arrival. **Don't pack items such as hats, gloves, boots, jackets and/or coats in checked baggage, since they may be required immediately on arrival.**

♦ WHEN THE AIRCRAFT DEPARTS THE GATE. It is highly advisable to remain at the boarding gate until you've been assured the aircraft is in flight and on its way. It is also advisable to call the airline within 30 minutes after departure to make certain the flight will be arriving on schedule at its destination. There have been occasions where a flight has had to return to its departure airport or divert to an alternate, so continue to check on the flight's progress by calling the airline for an update on its progress. (This information is usually provided on a recorded message.) Individuals meeting your child should also check this information.

♦ REMINDER FOR THE PERSON MEETING YOUR CHILD. To make certain that the individual meeting your child is the same person you have designated on the permission slip, he or she will be required to present a photo ID to the airline representative before your child will be released.

20

Senior Citizens

After flying airplanes for forty-nine years of which the last thirty was as a commercial airline captain, let's see what the airline industry has to offer my fellow senior citizens. *Hmmm, not bad.* It looks like the industry has covered all the bases for us. Since the majority of us are on a fixed income, (retirement and social security), the cost of air travel is one of our considerations.

Nine major airlines offer discount books. The exceptions are Southwest and AirTran Airlines.

♦ **America West**
62 years of age; 4 tickets/ $549; 14 days in advance; travel restrictions apply.

♦ **American**
62 years of age; 4 tickets/ $596;14 days in advance; good for all 48 states + Hawaii and some Caribbean locations; no blackout during holidays; travel 7 days a week, Hawaii requires 2 tickets each way.

♦ **Continental**
62 years of age;4 tickets/ $579; 8 tickets/ $1,079; 14 days in advance; travel restrictions apply.

♦ **Delta**
62 years of age; 4 tickets/ $596; 14 days in advance; good for all 48 states, no travel to Mexico.

♦ **Northwest**
65 years of age; 4 tickets/ $540; 14 days in advance; travel restrictions apply.

♦ **Southwest**
65 years of age; no discount books; discounts offered on individual tickets.

♦ **Trans World Airlines**
62 years of age; 4 tickets/ $548; Hawaii requires 2 tickets each way; blackouts apply.

♦ **United**

62 years of age; 4 tickets/$596; 14 days in advance; good in all 48 states and Hawaii; 2 tickets to and from Hawaii; Holiday restrictions apply to Hawaii.

♦ **US Airways**

62 years of age; 4 tickets/ $596; 14 days in advance; good in all 48 states Canada and some Caribbean locations; no blackout dates.

It is highly recommended you make reservations **well in advance** since there are very few senior citizen seats available.

Since seats are limited, it is wise to purchase these tickets through your Travel Agent to allow for a personalized reservation selection. Your Agent will collect the cost of the tickets and issue you a voucher to exchange at the airline ticket counter for the ticket booklet.

NOTE: Be sure and check with your Travel Agent, Occasionally airlines have promotional fares that are cheaper than Senior Citizen fares.

21

Airline Clubs

Frequent flyers that spend many hours waiting for their flights should avail themselves of the peace, privacy and quiet of Private Airline Clubs. These are usually located in airline terminals of most large cities.

Services and amenities may include free local phone calls, private meeting rooms, fax machines, personal computer terminals, PC printers and copiers, liquor service and complimentary coffee, tea and snacks. In certain US cities and most foreign countries, liquor service is complimentary.

Most airlines will allow you to sample its hospitality by purchasing a one-day pass for a small fee. (Some will issue a complimentary one-time pass).

IF you like what they offer, which you will, you may apply for a yearly or lifetime membership. These costs vary from $100 a year to $3,000 for lifetime memberships.

America West Airlines - The Phoenix Club, 2 locations plus 13 affiliated clubs worldwide. $200 per year individual membership- $75 additional with spouse card. For information call 1-602-693-2994.

American Airlines - The Admirals Club, established 1939. 46 locations around the world. $350 per year first time members- $250 to renew- $250 additional for spouse card.

No lifetime memberships. May substitute AAdvantage Miles in lieu of cash.

One-day guest pass (good for a 24-hour period) is available at $50, two guests at domestic clubs, one guest at international clubs. $50 fee will be credited within 60 days towards membership. For information call 1-800-237-7971.

Continental Airlines - The Presidents Club, established 30+ years. 15 locations worldwide plus numerous affiliated clubs worldwide. $200 per year first time members- $75 additional with spouse card. Lifetime member $1,825- $2500 with spouse. For information call 1-800-322-2640.

Delta Airlines - Crown Room Club, located in over 40 cities across North America. $300 per year first time members- $100 additional with spouse card. No lifetime memberships. May substitute Sky Miles in lieu of cash. For information contact Delta Airlines-Crown Room Club Membership Center-P.O. Box 102171- Atlanta, GA 30368- 2171.

Northwest Airlines - World Clubs, 26 locations worldwide. $270 per year first time members- $95 additional with spouse card. Lifetime member $2950- $1600 additional with spouse card. For information call 1-800-692-3788.

Southwest Airlines - Do not offer club memberships.

Trans World Airlines - Ambassadors Club, 26 locations worldwide. $175 per year first time members- $75 additional with spouse card. Lifetime member $1900- $500 additional with spouse card. One time guest pass is available, must call customer service at 1-800-527-1468 for arrangements and information.

United Airlines - The Red Carpet Club, over 40 clubrooms around the world. Membership prices vary with the amount of mileage you fly on United each year, from $400 to $175 per year for single membership- from $650 to $275 per year with spouse card. May substitute Mileage Plus in lieu of cash. For information call 1-520-881-0500.

US Airways - US Airways Club, located in 27 cities across North America. Individual membership $250 per year- $75 additional with spouse card. Lifetime membership $2950- $1600 additional with spouse card. A one-day pass is available for $25 and will be credited that day towards membership. For information call 1-800-828-8522.

Priority Pass - A network of over 200 airport lounges in virtually every major airport in the world. Participants consist of independently operated airport lounges as well as eight (8) airline lounge programs, i.e. Aces, AeroMexico, America West, Continental, Gulf Air, Kuwait Airways, Northwest and Trans World Airlines. Priority Pass is a perfect complement to an existing airline airport lounge membership, or as a stand-alone program. Membership fees range from $99 to $295 per year.

For information call 1-800-352-2834.

I strongly recommend membership in Priority Pass to Frequent Fliers, Domestic and International as an outstanding value.

22

Transporting Pets

"Cancel my reservations! If I can't take my baby I'm not going."

When planning a trip many pet owners are faced with the difficult decision of leaving their cat or dog in a kennel or sending their pet on a flight as checked baggage.

Well, depending on the size of your pet, you now have an alternate means of taking Kitty or Fido on your flight, thanks to efforts of Gayle Martz, a TWA flight attendant who discovered that her beloved pet, a Lhasa Apso named Sherpa, was not as welcome aboard airplanes as she.

For Ms. Martz, animal lover, this was a problem. Her successful efforts to get airlines to modify their onboard pet policy have allowed passengers to take their smaller pets in the cabin with them.

Air Canada, Alaska, America West, American, Continental, Delta, Northwest, TWA, Pan Am, United and **US Airways** now allow you to carry your small pet on the airplane to be placed under the seat in front of you. Each airline has their own rules and restrictions on the number of pets to be carried on each flight, the size of the pet bag and cost of transporting them. The cost of transporting a pet varies from $40 to $60.

When making your reservation check with your Travel Agent for information.

Because of the limit placed on the number of pets allowed on each flight, make a reservation for your pet as far in advance as possible.

If your pet meets the airlines carry-on criteria, Ms. Martz recommends you follow her well-researched recommendations:

♦ **Maintain a low profile.**
♦ **Do not take your pet out of the bag.**

Pets in the passenger cabin are a privilege, which could be taken away if we violate these rules.

Ms. Martz manufactures an airline approved soft-sided pet carrier that is designed to fit under the airline seats. Contact the Sherpa Pet Trading Company (800) 743-7723, Fax 212- 308-1187, Web Site www.sherpapet.com for information.

If your pet is large, (over 20 lb.) the airline will accommodate he/she in the heated and ventilated cargo compartment.

TRAVEL TIPS FOR PETS:

♦ **Plan Ahead:** Make reservations in advance.

♦ **Airline Restrictions:** Make sure to check if there are any special policies that you must adhere to. Rules, regulations and charges vary from airline to airline.

♦ **Carry-on Bags:** These must be soft sided, like Martz' Sherpa Bag, allowing for your pet to fit comfortably under the seat in front of you and have room to stand up and turn around within the bag.

♦ **Absorbent Liners:** Airlines insist pet carriers have an absorbent liner. You can use a towel.

♦ **Health Certificate:** Be sure to carry a current health certificate, issued by your veterinarian within seven to 10 days prior to your flight. This certificate should include all inoculations your pet has had.

♦ **Tranquilizers:** Many veterinarians recommend **not** tranquilizing your pet as the medication may inhibit sweating and can make your pet sick. Tranquilizers may remove an animal's natural ability to protect itself and reduce its survival instinct. Play it smart: check with Your veterinarian about Your pet.

◆ **Feeding:** It is best to feed your pet lightly when traveling. I recommend food be offered approximately six hours before flight time in order to prevent airsickness. Take the water dish away at two hours before flight time. (You can offer an ice cube or two during the trip.)

◆ **Walking Your Traveler:** Before entering the terminal take your friend for a stroll, but not near the entrance of other travelers.

◆ **Comfort Your Friend:** If you sense your little companion getting excited, reach into the bag and stroke gently. Do not take him/her out of the bag.

◆ **Stay Calm:** Your pet will react to your mood.

23

Tips from the Cockpit

◆ For your convenience use a travel agent when making a reservation.

◆ Take a non-stop flight if available.

◆ When traveling to the airport use a personal vehicle if possible.

◆ Have a Skycap check your luggage at curbside.

◆ Keep your personal carry-on items close to you and in sight at all times.

◆ Make sure you have a Government-issued picture ID in your possession.

◆ Never make any comment, even in jest, about hijacking, bombs or weapons.

◆ Wait for your seat row to be announced before boarding aircraft.

◆ Pay close attention to the emergency instructions - your life may depend on it.

◆ Keep your seat belt fastened while seated. Move about only when necessary.

- When making reservations, check if meals are offered.
- Deplane in an orderly fashion; don't rush the exit.
- Arrive at baggage claim as soon as possible to be there when your bags arrive.
- Let Skycaps retrieve your luggage to prevent personal injury.

24

Airline Terminology

A

ABORT - to stop the forward motion of the aircraft during take off, to terminate the takeoff

AIR-SPEED - the forward motion of an aircraft, as shown on an air-speed indicator located in the cockpit

AIR TRAFFIC CONTROLLERS - highly trained individuals who direct the flow of aircraft on the ground and in the air

AIRWAYS - a designated track which an aircraft follows in flight, (a road)

ALTIMETER - an indicator in the cockpit which displays the height above the surface

APPROACH AND DEPARTURE CONTROL - air-traffic controllers directing the flow of traffic approaching and departing an airport

APU - auxiliary power unit is a turbine engine which supplies air-conditioning and electrical power for the aircraft on the ground when the engines are shut down; also supplies air pressure to assist in starting jet engines

ATC - air traffic control; the process of controlling air traffic

ATIS - automatic terminal information service, a broadcast of recorded information of essential but routine information, i.e., weather, runway in use, altimeter setting

AUTOPILOT - an electronic device that controls the vertical and lateral guidance of an aircraft automatically

AWARDS - gratuity for using the services of an airline

B

BOARDING PASS - a document issued to a passenger to allow boarding of the aircraft; it may also indicate the passenger's seat assignment

C

CABIN - the interior of the aircraft

CEILING - the measured distance between the bottom of the clouds and the runway surface

CENTERLINE LIGHTS - flush in ground lights in the center of the runway spaced in 50 foot increments; on takeoff or landing the runway centerline lights are white until the last 3000 feet of the runway, white lights alternate with red for the next 2000 feet,

and turn red for the last 1000 feet of runway
CHOP - turbulence reported in flight, light or moderate, light- hardly any noticeable discomfort, moderate- slight discomfort aircraft is experiencing small variations in altitude and heading

CLEAR AIR TURBULENCE - CAT- turbulence especially associated with jet aircraft flying above 15000 feet; there are no visual cues to warn the pilot of this condition, therefore relying on pilot reports from other aircraft in the area (PIREPS)

CLEARANCE DELIVERY - a radio transmission providing a pilot with altitude, heading and the route he or she may be expected to fly, this information is normally provided to a flight while at the boarding gate, prior to engine start

CROSSING TRAFFIC - traffic in flight passing from left to right or right to left

D

DEREGULATION - a change in law permitting free entry into the market

DISPATCH - licensed professionals who monitor and track the progress of a flight, to enhance its safety and efficiency

F

FIX - a geographic position in flight

FLAPS - a moveable section of a wing that provides lift and drag, most are located on the rear of the wing (trailing edge)

FLIGHT ATTENDANTS - flight crew members whose primary duty is the safety of the passengers, and secondarily, to provide service for the passengers' comfort

FLIGHT DISPATCHERS - (see dispatch).

FLIGHT LEVEL - an altitude above 17000 feet assigned to an aircraft, i.e., 18000 feet-FL 180 35000 feet -FL 350 (three five zero)

FLOW CONTROL - the in trail spacing of aircraft to allow for little or no delays on arrival at your destination airport

FREQUENT FLYER - a passenger who flies a particular airline often

G

GATE CHANGE - a departure gate assigned to your flight different from the original assigned gate that was posted earlier

GROUND CONTROL - an air traffic controller who issues advisories to aircraft moving on the ground

GROUND-SPEED - the speed which an aircraft moves over the ground, air-speed plus or minus wind speed, i.e., 300 miles per hour air-speed minus 50 mile per hour head wind = 250 miles per hour ground speed, (see air-speed)

H

HIGH SPEED TAXIWAY - an exit leaving a runway that's angled to allow for a faster than normal speed leaving the runway

HOLDING - a procedure which allows the air-traffic controllers to sequence aircraft when delays are experienced in flight, usually a series of turns at a fix (see fix)

I

IN FLIGHT DELAYS - may be accomplished by having the aircraft reduce its cruising speed, may be issued turns, (360 degree), or be required to hold (see holding)

IN TRAIL SPACING - (see flow control)

J

JETWAY - a planing and deplaning walkway allowing passengers access to and from an aircraft without being exposed to the elements; may be movable or a fixed position jetway

L

LANDING GEAR - the wheels and their supporting structures, which retract and extend, and are housed inside the aircraft in flight

M

MACH - an indication of speed relative to the speed of sound at a given altitude, mach 1 being the equivalent to the speed of sound, mach .75, 75% the speed of sound, etc.

MISSED APPROACH- when an aircraft must abandon its approach and landing as directed by air traffic control or the pilot in command for safety reasons, i.e. inclement weather, aircraft or vehicles on the runway

MODERATE - when referred to as a level of turbulence light, moderate, severe (see chop)

N

NOISE ABATEMENT - a take-off and landing procedure custom designed for a particular airport to alleviate excessive noise associated with aircraft engines, over noise sensitive areas

NOSE WHEEL STEERING - a device used by the pilot to maneuver the aircraft on the ground similar to an automobile steering wheel

O

OVERHEAD STORAGE - an area above the passengers' seats for storage of personal effects

P

PRESSURIZATION - the use of compressors to increase air pressure in an airplane cabin which allows for flight at altitudes without the use of an oxygen mask. The compressors are an integral part of the aircraft's engines. As the aircraft begins its climb from a airport at sea level the aircraft compressors will supply compressed air into the relatively air tight cabin. A modern jet liner's cabin will stay at sea level pressure until the aircraft is at approximately 17000 feet, then the cabin pressure will begin to increase to approximately 9000 feet as the aircraft climbs to its cruising altitude

PSR - Passenger Service Representative- an airline employee who assists passengers with their needs, (questions, directions, etc.)

PUSH-BACK - moving the aircraft from the gate away from the jetway to allow the aircraft to start its engines and taxi away from the terminal with sufficient obstruction clearance

R

RADAR VECTORS - a service provided by air traffic control for in-flight separation

RAMP - the area around the terminal where the aircraft park

RESERVATIONS - employees of an airline offering telephone information to prospective customers

REVERSE THRUST - reducing the forward speed of an aircraft by employing thrust deflection devices on the engines

RUNWAYS - take-off and landing areas located on airports, aligned with compass headings, Runway 36L, the north runway- 360 degrees- on the left side of the airport, i.e., 36L, 36C, 36R, left, center, or right

S

SECURITY - a procedure one must accomplish prior to entering the aircraft boarding area to eliminate the possibility of restricted items being carried on the aircraft

SERVICE FEES - monetary fees charged to passengers by travel agents to cover their cost of issuing a airline ticket when they are not compensated by the airline

SEVERE - reference to as a level of turbulence, (see chop)

SIMULATOR - a training device to teach and maintain proficiency of pilots

SKY CAP - personnel who provide luggage service to passengers, usually are not employed by the airline

SLATS - aerodynamic lift and drag devices usually located on the forward leading edge of the wing

SPOILERS GROUND AND FLIGHT - panel like devices located on the top side of the wing that reduce the aerodynamic lift of the wing, in flight they raise to an angle of about 45 degrees allowing the aircraft to slow and increase its rate of descent, on the ground they extend to almost vertical allowing for the full weight of the aircraft to settle on the landing gear for more effective braking by reducing the lift on the wing

T

TAXIWAY - a network of roadways by which an aircraft proceeds to or from a runway or parking area

TOWER - a glass enclosed facility on the airport which allows air traffic controllers to monitor and inform aircraft in their area of issues vital to their safety

TRAFFIC - pilot, controller phraseology for other aircraft

TRAVEL AGENT - professional travel experts who assist the traveling public in making all their travel arrangements

TUG - a vehicle that attaches to the front wheels, nose gear, and pulls or pushes an aircraft to a predetermined position so it can taxi clear of all obstructions

TV MONITORS - videos placed throughout the airline terminal which supply information to passengers, departure and arrival gates and times, etc.

V

VISIBILITY - the horizontal distance one can see

V_2 - an airspeed at which an aircraft lifts off the runway

V_R - a speed at which an aircraft begins its rotation in preparation for liftoff (V_2)

W

WAKE TURBULENCE - a disturbed area of turbulent air created by vortices from one or more aircraft, may be encountered in flight or on the ground during take-off and landing

WHEEL WELLS - an area located in the aircraft's underside where the landing gear is stored when retracted after take-off

25

Airline Reservation and Service Numbers

Quick Reference Domestic Airlines Reservation Numbers

Air Canada	(800) 776-3000
Air Midwest	(800) 428-4322
Air Nevada	(800) 634-6377
Air Wisconsin	(800) 241-6522
AirTran	(800) 247-8726
Alaska Airlines	(800) 426-0333
Aloha Airlines	(800) 367-5250
Aloha Island Air	(808) 828-0806
America West Airlines	(800) 292-9378
American Airlines	(800) 433-7300
Bahamas Air	(800) 222-4262
Carnival Airlines	(800) 437-2110
Cayman Airways	(800) 422-9626

Continental Airlines	(800) 525-0280
Continental Express	(713) 985-2600
Delta Airlines	(800) 221-1212
Hawaiian Airlines	(800) 367-5320
Mexicana Airlines	(800) 531-7921
Midwest Express Airlines	(800) 452-2022
New York Helicopter	(800) 645-3494
Northwest Airlines	(800) 225-2525
Pan American Airways	(800) 359-7262
Reno Air	(800) 736-6247
Southwest Airlines	(800) 531-5600
Tower Air	(800) 348-6937
Trans World Airlines (Domestic)	(800) 221-2000
Trans World Airlines (lnt'l)	(800) 892-4141
Trans World Express	(800) 221-2000
United Airlines	(800) 241-6522
US Airways	(800) 428-4322

Other Airlines

Aer Lingus	(800) 223-6537
Aeroflot Soviet Airlines	(800) 995-5555
Air France	(800) 237-2747
Air India	(212) 751-6200
Air Jamaica	(800) 523-5585
Air New Zealand	(800) 262-1234
Alitalia Airlines	(800) 223-5730
All Nippon Airways	(800) 235-9262

ALM Antillean Airlines	(800) 327-7197
Ansett Australia Airlines	(800) 366-1300
Asiana Airlines	(800) 227-4262
Austrian Airlines	(800) 843-0002
Avianca Airlines	(800) 284-2622
British Airways	(800) 247-9297
BWIA Int'l	(800) 327-7401
Canadian Airlines Int'l	(800) 426-7000
Cathay Pacific	(800) 233-2742
China Airlines	(800) 227-5118
Egyptair	(800) 334-6787
EL Al Israel Airlines	(800) 223-6700
Iberia Airlines	(800) 772-4642
Japan Airlines	(800) 525-3663
KLM Royal Dutch Airlines	(800) 374-7747
Korean Airlines	(800) 438-5000
LACSA Airline of Costa Rica	(800) 225-2272
Lan Chile Airlines	(800) 735-5526
Lufthansa German Airlines	(800) 645-3880
Olympic Airways	(800) 223-1226
Qantas Airways	(800) 227-4500
Sabena World Airlines	(800) 955-2000
Scandinavian Airlines	(800) 221-2350
Singapore Airlines	(800) 742-3333
South African Airways	(800) 722-9675
Swissair	(800) 221-4750
Varig Brazilian	(800) 468-2744
Virgin Atlantic	(800) 862-8621

The following information provided by the
INTERNATIONAL AIRLINE PASSENGERS
ASSOCIATION

International Airline Passengers Association
Safety Hotline
P.O. Box 700188
Dallas, TX 75370-0188
800/821-4272
Monday - Friday. 9am - 11am (non-members)

FAA
Office of Public Affairs
800 Independence Avenue, SW
Washington, DC 20591
900/322-7873 (Consumer Complaints)
800/255-1111 (Safety Hotline)

Department of Transportation
400 7th Street, SW
Washington, DC 20590
202/366-2220 (Air Travel Consumer Complaints)

ALASKA AIRLINES
P.O. Box 68900
Seattle, WA 98168-0900
206/439-4477
206/431-7425 (lost luggage)

AMERICAN AIRLINES
Customer Relations
P.O. Box 619612 MD 2400
DFW Airport, TX 75261-9612
817/967-2000
800/535-5225 (lost luggage)

CONTINENTAL AIRLINES
Customer Relations
3663 Sam Houston Pkwy.
Houston, TX 77032
713/834-5000
800/525-0280 (lost luggage call res.)

DELTA AIRLINES
Consumer Affairs
Box 20706
Hartsfield lnt'I Airport
Atlanta, GA 30320
404/715-2600
800/325-8224 (lost luggage)

NORTHWEST AIRLINES
Consumer Affairs
5101 Northwest Drive
St Paul, MN 55111-3034
612/726-2046
800/648-4897 (lost luggage)

SOUTHWEST AIRLINES
Customer Relations
P.O. Box 36611
Dallas, TX 75235
214/792-4223
214/904-4000 (lost luggage)

TWA
Consumer Relations
100 S. Bedford Rd.
Mt Kisco, NY 10549
800/325-4815
800/221-2000 (lost luggage)

UNITED AIRLINES
Customer Relations
P.O. Box 66100
Chicago, IL 60666
847/700-6796
800/221-6903 (lost luggage)

US AIRWAYS
Consumer Affairs
P.O. Box 1501
Winston-Salem, NC 27102-1501
910/661-0061
800/371-4771 (lost luggage)

26

Travel Web Sites

The following is a selection of Internet WEB SITES, which will allow you to select a travel professional.

You may choose from thousands of Travel Agents, and the major Airlines.

The Association of Retail Travel Agents, (ARTA)–

http://www.waveconcepts.com/ARTA/index.html

American Society of Travel Agents, (ASTA) –

http://www.astanet.com/

- **America West**
  http://www.americawest.com/splash.htm
- **American**
  http://www.americanair.com/
- **Continental**
  http://www.flycontinental.com
- **Delta**
  http://www.delta-air.com/index.html
- **Northwest**
  http://www.nwa.com/
- **Pan American**
  http://www.pan-american.com/
- **Southwest**
  http://www.iflyswa.com/
- **TWA**
  http://www.twa.com/
- **United**
  http://www.ual.com/home/default.htm
- **US Airways**
  http://www.usair.com/

All Airlines
http://www.travelpage.com/air/airlines.htm

http://pages.prodigy.com/airport/air2.htm

http://www.redbay.com/sjipp/html/airline_links.html

27

Seat Selection Guide

Recommendations when making seat selections:

There are three basic jet transport designs commonly used by the major airlines - those whose engines are located under the wings, those that are on or near the tail of the aircraft, or a combination of both.

When making a seat selection consider the following:

Noise, vibration, location of entrance and exit doors (normal), closets, lavatories, galleys, location of exit doors, windows and equipment (emergency).

NOISE - On jet powered aircraft the front is usually the quietest, and on propeller driven aircraft the rear is generally quieter. Prior to jet airliners, first class passengers were seated in the rear of the aircraft.

On under wing mounted engines, noise is greatest at the rear of the wing. i.e., Boeing 737,757, 767 and 777.

On tail mounted engines, noise is greatest in the last rows of the aircraft. i.e., Boeing 727, DC9 and MD80.

On aircraft that have both under wing and tail mounted engines, it would then be obvious that the area of greatest noise would extend from the rear of the wing to the tail. i.e., DC10, MD11 and L1011.

VIBRATION - Increases as you move to the rear. Usually noticeable from the wing to the tail of the aircraft. Very noticeable during approach and landing due to the extension of the landing gear, slats and flaps.

ENTRANCES and EXITS (NORMAL) - Seating adjacent to these will make entering and exiting convenient.

CLOSETS - They are few and far between on most aircraft, so don't plan on finding space in these.

LAVATORIES - If a passenger has a physical condition that requires seating in close proximity of a lavatory, I recommend not sitting within several rows of the lavatory, or on the aisle adjacent to them, due to the possibility of passengers standing in the aisle, especially on long flights.

GALLEYS - Passengers seated near a galley may be served first if a meal service is offered. One can expect increased flight attendant activity in this area, with associated noise and food preparation odors.

EXITS (EMERGENCY) - Even though the possibility is remote, of a passenger ever having to use these, locating and sitting at or in close proximity of an emergency exit is an excellent choice. WARNING - These exits may be very large and heavy. **If you sit at an emergency exit you must be physically and mentally capable of this task.** REMEMBER - Your life and that of your fellow passengers are in your hands if these exits must be used during an emergency.

EMERGENCY EQUIPMENT - Passengers should know the location of emergency equipment in the passenger cabin. i.e., water and chemical fire extinguishers crash axes, life rafts, personal flotation devices, flashlights, and oxygen masks.

The aircraft interior depicted on the right is a Boeing 777-200 configured to accommodate 328 passengers.

There are 24 First Class Seats at a 60-inch pitch, 61 Business Class Seats at a 38-inch pitch and 243 Economy Class Seats at a 32-inch pitch.

(PITCH- The distance between a given point on your seat to the exact same point on the seat in front or back of yours. i.e. from the front of your arm-rest to the front of the arm-rest on the seat in front or in back of you).

Aircraft interior arrangements are configured to the individual airline specifications.

The 777 is powered by two under wing mounted engines.

Boeing 777-200

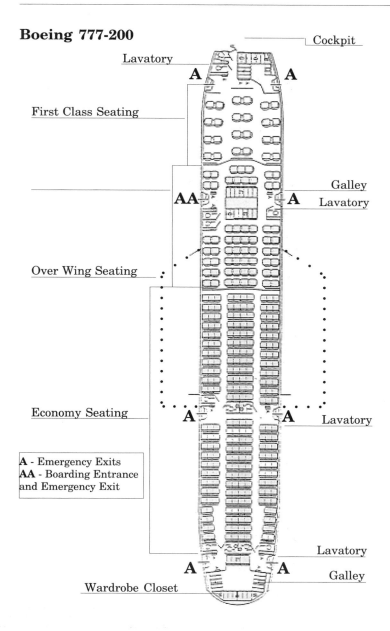

Cockpit

Lavatory

A   **A**

First Class Seating

Galley

AA   **A**   Lavatory

Over Wing Seating

Economy Seating   **A**   **A**   Lavatory

A - Emergency Exits
AA - Boarding Entrance
and Emergency Exit

Lavatory

A   **A**   Galley

Wardrobe Closet

28

Typical Flight Procedures

The following diagrams are a generalization of normal in flight procedures. Actual in flight procedures may vary from airline to airline.

133

Typical Location of Aircraft Flight Controls

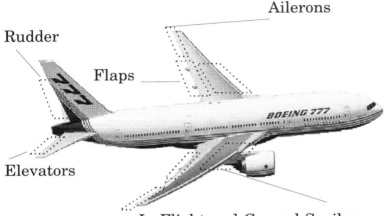

Ailerons

Rudder

Flaps

Elevators

In-Flight and Ground Spoilers

Ailerons - Banks Aircraft left or right

Rudder - Controls lateral movement of aircraft

Elevators - Pitches aircraft up or down

Flaps - Provides more "Lift" at slower speeds (Used on takeoffs and landings).

Spoilers - In flight; reduces the aerodynamic lift of the wing, allows the aircraft to slow and increase its rate of descent. On the ground; allows for the full weight of the aircraft to settle on the landing gear for more effective braking.

Typical Take-off and Departure Procedure

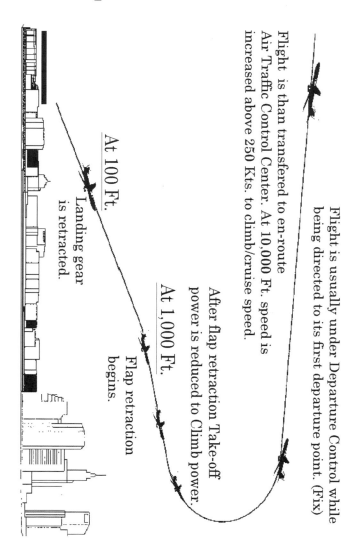

Flight is usually under Departure Control while being directed to its first departure point. (Fix)

Flight is than transfered to en-route Air Traffic Control Center. At 10,000 Ft. speed is increased above 250 Kts. to climb/cruise speed.

At 100 Ft.

Landing gear is retracted.

At 1,000 Ft.

Flap retraction begins.

After flap retraction Take-off power is reduced to Climb power.

Typical Noise Abatement Take-off and Departure Procedure

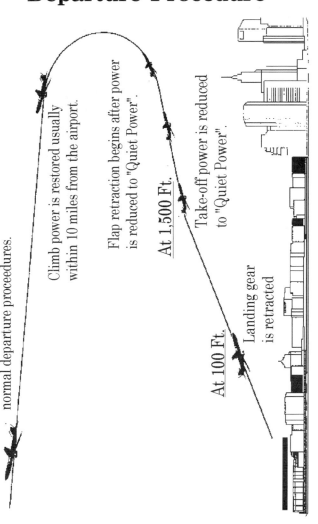

Flight continues according to normal departure proceedures.

Climb power is restored usually within 10 miles from the airport.

Flap retraction begins after power is reduced to "Quiet Power".

At 1,500 Ft.

Take-off power is reduced to "Quiet Power".

Landing gear is retracted

At 100 Ft.

Typical Arrival and Landing Procedure

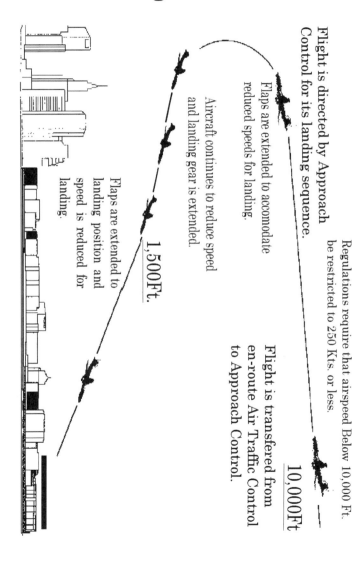

Flight is directed by Approach Control for its landing sequence.

Regulations require that airspeed Below 10,000 Ft. be restricted to 250 Kts. or less.

Flaps are extended to accomodate reduced speeds for landing.

Flight is transfered from en-route Air Traffic Control to Approach Control.

Aircraft continues to reduce speed and landing gear is extended.

10,000Ft

Flaps are extended to landing position and speed is reduced for landing.

1,500Ft.

Typical In-Flight
Holding Procedure

(Right turns, left turns may
be assigned by Air Traffic Control)

Electronic Navigational
Intersection.

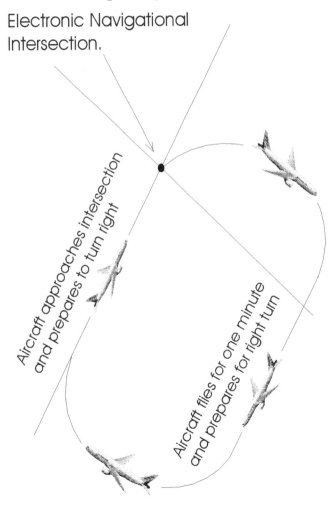

Aircraft approaches intersection
and prepares to turn right

Aircraft flies for one minute
and prepares for right turn

Index

Order Form

⚐ Fax orders: (305) 296-3334

☎ Telephone orders Call Toll Free: 1 (877) FLY-ING1
Have your credit card ready.

✉ Postal orders: FSH Publishing, Box 4293
                       Key West, FL 33041-4293

☐ Please send the *Flying Smart Handbook* to me.

Company name: _____

Name: _____

Address: _____

City: _____ State: _____ Zip: ____ - ____

Telephone: (____) _____

Sales tax:
Please add 7% for books shipped to Florida addresses.

Shipping:
$4.00 for the first book and $2.00 for each additional book.

Payment:
☐ Cheque
☐ Credit cards: ☐ VISA, ☐ MasterCard ☐ Amex ☐ Discover

Card number: _____

Name on card: _____ Exp. date: ____ / ____

Call *toll free* and order now

Order Form

▰ Fax orders: (305) 296-3334

☎ Telephone orders Call Toll Free: 1 (877) FLY-ING1
Have your credit card ready.

✉ Postal orders: FSH Publishing, Box 4293
Key West, FL 33041-4293

❑ Please send the *Flying Smart Handbook* to me.

Company name: _____

Name:_____

Address:_____

City: _____ State:_____ Zip:_____-_____

Telephone: (___) _____

Sales tax:
Please add 7% for books shipped to Florida addresses.

Shipping:
$4.00 for the first book and $2.00 for each additional book.

Payment:
❑ Cheque
❑ Credit cards: ❑VISA, ❑ MasterCard ❑Amex ❑Discover

Card number:_____

Name on card: _____ Exp. date:_____/_____

Call *toll free* and order now